D0719039

7000373041 8X

The Brewer's Tale

Memoirs of a Master Brewer

Frank Priestley

Merlin Unwin Books

First published in Great Britain by Merlin Unwin Books, 2010

Copyright © Frank Priestley 2010

All rights reserved, including the right to reproduce this book
or portions thereof in any form or by any means, electronic or
mechanical, including photocopying, recording, or by any
information storage and retrieval system, without permission in
writing from the publisher. All inquiries should be addressed to
Merlin Unwin Books.

Published by:
Merlin Unwin Books Ltd
Palmers House
7 Corve Street
Ludlow
Shropshire SY8 1DB
U.K.

www.merlinunwin.co.uk

The author asserts his moral right to be identified with this work.

Designed and set in Bembo by Merlin Unwin
Printed in Great Britain by Cromwell Press Group, Trowbridge

ISBN 978 1 906122 17 1

To Jane, Dan and John – who have
made my life complete.

Also published by Merlin Unwin Books

The Tippling Philosopher
Jeremy James

Maynard: Adventures of a Bacon Curer
Maynard Davies

Maynard: Secrets of a Bacon Curer
Maynard Davies

Manual of a Traditional Bacon Curer
Maynard Davies

Hedgerow Medicine
Julie & Matthew Bruton-Seal

Contents

1

The Banner Cross Hotel

On 20 September 1940, I was born in a house at Banner Cross in Sheffield which had the good fortune to stand next to a pub, the *Banner Cross Hotel*. Some 64 years earlier, the row of dwellings which included my home had witnessed the murder of Arthur Dyson by the notorious Victorian criminal, Charlie Peace. It was believed that Peace had 'become enamoured' of Mrs Dyson and when her husband had tried to chase him off, he had shot Dyson in the head, for his trouble. But I had little time to worry about any of this because by the time I was three months old, Adolf Hitler had decided to flatten the city and the Sheffield Blitz began. Mercifully, our house and the pub were spared the bombardment. The closest bomb fell in a nearby quarry. The whole house shook from the explosion.

As I grew up, I shared the back bedroom with my younger brother Jim. I have memories of lying awake on summer nights listening to the sounds of laughter, merriment and music floating up from the open windows of the pub. Someone played the popular songs of the time on a piano while others joined in with the words. The later the evening, the more enthusiastic the singers became until at last a voice of authority would call out, 'Time gentlemen, please.' I was too young then to understand what a dreadful and dreaded phrase this was.

The pub became a place of mystery to me. I could not see in the frosted windows – windows that bore the words, 'Duncan Gilmore', the name of a now-forgotten brewer. Children were not allowed inside the premises, but there was still a way that a child could sometimes catch a glimpse of this forbidden place during the daylight hours.

A door marked 'Off Sales' led to a small lobby which was dominated by a large wooden counter. Above this was a small hatch which, in turn, looked in on the serving area of the pub. If I could scavenge a few empty beer bottles from uncles or grandparents, I was allowed to take them to the Off Sales to collect the penny or halfpenny that was refunded on each one – bottles being returnable in those days. And while the landlady was sorting them out, I could gaze through at the now silent lounge and relish its unfamiliar, hop-laden, beery atmosphere. (In the years to come, I was destined to become very familiar with the aromas of hops, beer and public houses.)

I was educated at Nether Edge Grammar School, which was housed in a building that had once been used as a workhouse – and still was, according to some of its pupils. After 'O' levels, I concentrated on the sciences, physics, chemistry and biology, largely because that was what my friends were doing. They wanted to be things like dentists and pharmacists. I had no idea what I wanted to be. When the 'A' level results came out, I found that I had passed only physics and failed the other two. While my friends went to college, I went to the youth employment office to get a job.

What sort of a job would I like, asked the man behind the desk? (This was the late fifties, a time of full employment.) I had quite enjoyed the practical aspect of my recent studies so I told him that I would like to work in a laboratory. He pulled a file from the drawer and told me that he had three such jobs: one in the steelworks, one in a paint factory and one in a brewery. I didn't fancy the steelworks, even though my father and several of my uncles worked there. I had seen what it was like on a school trip and I was not impressed by the noise, smoke, dirt and danger in spite of the fact that I was told that it would be 'a job for life'. I didn't like the smell of paint either, so I opted for the brewery.

I was directed down to the site, interviewed within the hour and a few days later, I received a letter informing me that I had been appointed to the post of laboratory assistant (or lavatory attendant, as my brother quipped), a position which commanded the princely salary of six pounds, five shillings per week.

2

Tennant Brothers' Brewery

On Monday morning, 24 August 1959, I walked through the great archway into the brewery of Mess'rs Tennant Brothers Limited to start my first day of paid work.

Once in the brewery yard, I looked up at the tall buildings around me. The brewery had been originally established in 1820 by Proctor & Company in what eventually became the Market Place. Twenty years later, in 1840, it came into the ownership of the Tennant family and was designated Tennant Brothers.

In 1852, the firm was given four months notice to quit their premises which were leased from the Duke of Norfolk. A new location was found on the banks of the River Don by Lady's Bridge. It was the site once occupied by Sheffield Castle which had been demolished in 1648, during the Civil War. In the few short months available, the new brewery was built and production was transferred to the new premises without the loss of a single day's brewing! How did the Victorians manage to do things like that?

Around 1890, Alfred Barnard, the famous Victorian writer on breweries and distilleries, visited Tennant's and found it an 'extensive and handsome brewery'. After a tour round the produc-

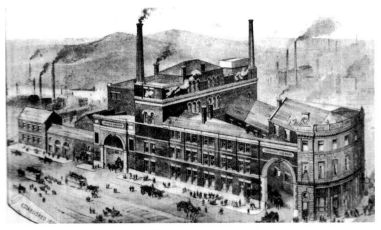

Tennant Brothers' Brewery in Sheffield.

tion areas, he was invited to sample the product. He was offered up to eight different beers.

Tennant's bitter beer, he found 'bright and sparkling with a tonic flavour'. Wharncliffe ale, which he seemed particularly drawn to, he described as 'a rich, full and invigorating beverage'. The brewery had been awarded a medal at the Beer Exhibition in 1873 and later a silver medal at the Albert Hall. (By the end of the century, Tennant Brothers' would become the biggest brewery in Sheffield.)

Barnard concluded by reporting : 'Of the stout and porter we can only speak in the highest praise, as they are quite equal to the London standard.' This was praise indeed as these beers were the speciality of the London brewers at that time.

Porter, like stout, was a very dark beer, having been brewed with roasted malts. It was intermediate in style between ale and stout but, unlike stout, a portion of partly fermented beer was added to it prior to leaving the brewery. The result of this was that porter had a rich, creamy head because the beer was still fermenting and as it still contained many nutrients, it was highly nourishing. Perhaps this is why it was so popular amongst London porters who are said to have given it its name.

True draught porter is not widely brewed these days but the name is sometimes used by older drinkers in Ireland to describe the much loved bitter stout brewed over there. I remember a Dublin man once saying to me:

'I don't care how expensive it gets, so long as it doesn't get scarce!'

In Barnard's day, the brewery had stabling for forty shire horses and some were used right up until 1950, with pairs pulling cask beer drays, and single horses pulling bottled beer. Their drivers claimed that in snowy weather, horses got through where lorries could not, on the many hills around Sheffield. The brewery had also used steam wagons in and around the town.

As I walked through the brewery, my nose was assailed by a confusion of different aromas, as yet unfamiliar to me. Eventually, I found the laboratory.

The Chief Chemist was Eric Wiles. I was soon to learn that this modest man was world famous in the brewing industry. I only learned this by noticing that he received mail from America, Japan and elsewhere, requesting details of his recent research.

Eric had made a detailed study of 'wild yeast'. This phrase referred to any strain of yeast, other than the one used in the brewery fermentation. Many of these wild yeasts could cause beer spoilage by changing the beer's flavour and aroma or by causing cloudiness. It was important to know where and how they were being introduced into the brewery. This work had stopped abruptly before I arrived on the scene. One of the 'old time' directors had pointed out to him that he was employed to carry out analysis for the brewery rather than to do his own private thing.

When I got to know him better, I asked Eric why he had never sought a research post at the Brewing Industry Research Foundation in Surrey or other such organizations that certainly would have welcomed him with open arms. He had thought about it, he said, but he would miss the atmosphere of a working brewery. At the time I was not impressed with his answer, but later I realised the wisdom of his words.

An important part of my duties as laboratory assistant was the analysis of the finished products. Samples were taken from every brew and tested for colour, clarity and gravity. At that time, Tennant's produced four draught beers and five bottled beers. The draught beers were: Bitter Beer (BB), Best Bitter Beer (BBB), Rock Ale, which was a dark, mild ale and Queen's Ale. Rock Ale probably originated at the Nottingham Brewery (see later). The Nottingham cellars had been excavated out of the solid rock on which the old town stood. Beers stored in the cellars were known as *Rock Ales*. Queen's Ale was a premium draught beer. It was a pale, hoppy beer with a good body. Its perfect balance of malty sweetness and the bitterness of the finest hops ensured that it was the best draught beer that I have ever tasted (and that is saying something).

Tennant's bottled beers were: Lion Pale Ale – a fine pale ale, Lion Brown Ale – enjoyed by older drinkers, Glucose Stout – a beautiful sweet stout, No.1 Barley Wine – an old fashioned drink and Gold Label Barley Wine – a pale, sparkling barley wine, about which I will elaborate later. Gold Label (together with Lion Pale Ale) had been awarded the 'Prix D'Excellence 1958' in Belgium, which was one of the most important brewing countries in the world at that time. Tennant's proudly displayed the words 'Prix D'Excellence' on street posters advertising the barley wine. However, due to a certain lack of familiarity with the pronunciation of the French language in those days, the drink was perceived, in some circles as a forerunner of viagra, which did no harm at all to its rocketing sales.

The brewery served about 700 public houses. This high number was due, in part, to the fact that other brewery companies had been acquired over the years, in Sheffield and Nottingham, Barnsley and Worksop. Recent acquisitions included Clarkson's Brewery, Barnsley in 1956 and Worksop and Redford Brewery, Worksop in 1958. Some production was still being carried out at the Worksop brewery when I arrived and samples of their draught beers, Best Bitter and Amber Ale, were sent regularly to the laboratory for analysis. However, very soon after this, the brewery was closed down and production was transferred to Tennant's, where the ordinary bitter (BB) was renamed Amber Ale and Worksop's bottled Don Jon ale was brewed and bottled on the Sheffield plant. Don Jon was a lovely, smooth beer and even after its transfer to Tennant's, the Worksop logo, a green cross imposed on an oak tree, was still displayed on the bottle label.

In addition to analysis of the finished products, tests were carried out throughout the brewing process. Most importantly, the raw materials were analysed on a regular basis. The water used for brewing (always called liquor) was checked for acidity, hardness and clarity. Different kinds of liquor produced beers of different character. Thus Burton-on-Trent with its hard water produced and became famous for its bitter beers. London, on the other hand, having soft water, produced more mellow beers.

Labels from the beers bottled at Tennant Brothers' and Nimmo's Breweries.

Clockwise from left: Don Jon Ale, Nimmo's Export Ale, No.1 Barley Wine and Lion Pale Ale.

Originally, most breweries brewed with water from their wells. However, as demand grew, they progressively changed over to taking water from the local water board which was usually purer than the well water and, as a result, was likely to produce a blander beer. The brewers countered this by 'treating' the water, that is, by returning the natural salts to the water in order to retain the traditional flavour and character of the beer. At the time, this led some mischievous characters to suggest that beer was now 'all chemicals'. This was clearly foolish.

Yeast was examined microscopically for its general state of health and for the presence of beer spoilage organisms, such as acid-producing bacteria.

Following the harvest, hops were analysed for the amount of bittering substances they contained. This could be assessed chemically, although an experienced person could gain a lot of information from a hand evaluation. A few hop cones were rubbed vigorously between the palms of the hands for a few seconds and then discarded. The smear of resin left behind was examined and smelled. Not only could one get an indication of the level of bitterness but, more importantly (in those days), it was a good and perhaps only indication of the delicacy of the hop's aroma. Head Brewers would use the results of these tests to decide which batches of hops to purchase for the coming year's brews.

Samples of malt from the brewery store were analysed throughout the year and samples from the maltsters were received and tested when the new season's malt was ready. Malt was made by soaking barley grains in water to encourage germination. When the shoots began to grow, the process was arrested by drying the grains in a kiln. This ensured that sufficient enzymes were produced which would later convert the starchy contents into malt sugar or maltose and this would eventually be fermented into alcohol.

The standard analysis of malt would show how much colour it would contribute to the beer, what yield of beer could be expected and how much moisture there was in it. (Brewers did not like paying good money for water.) One of the most important aspects of malt was its nitrogen content. This was a measure of how much protein there was present. Contrary to what one might believe, protein is not to be encouraged in beer.

It is a rather unstable compound and while it might sit quite comfortably in a clear liquid one minute, a shift in conditions such as a temperature change can cause it to come out of solution and form a dense and unsightly haze. This is not a characteristic to be desired and therefore low nitrogen malts were produced for brewing. Even if it meant a lower yield, fertilizers were discouraged in the cultivation of brewing barleys. It was said that ideally, such barleys should be grown on land that had been fertilized for a previous crop. Slightly higher nitrogen malts could however be used in whisky distilleries, as the protein would be left behind after the distillation process.

For a beautiful and poetical description of the cultivation, malting and brewing of barley, there is none better than the poem by Robert Burns, *John Barleycorn*.

There were three kings into the east,
Three kings both great and high,
An' they hae sworn a solemn oath
John Barleycorn should die.

They took a plough and plough'd him down,
Put clods upon his head,
And they hae sworn a solemn oath
John Barleycorn was dead.

But cheerful spring came kindly on,
And showers began to fall;
John Barleycorn got up again,
And sore surpris'd them all.

The sultry suns of summer came,
And he grew thick and strong,
His head weel arm'd wi' pointed spears,
That no one should him wrong.

The sober autumn enter'd mild,
When he grew wan and pale;
His bending joints and drooping head
Shew'd he began to fail.

His colour sicken'd more and more,
He faded into age;
And then his enemies began
To shew their deadly rage.

They've taen a weapon long and sharp,
And cut him by the knee;
Then ty'd him fast upon a cart,
Like a rogue for forgerie.

They laid him down upon his back,
And cudgell'd him full sore;
They hung him up before the storm,
And turn'd him o'er and o'er.

They filled up a darksome pit,
With water to the brim,
They heaved in John Barleycorn,
There let him sink or swim.

They laid him out upon the floor,
To work him further woe,
And still as signs of life appear'd,
They toss'd him to and fro.

They wasted o'er a scorching flame,
The marrow of his bones;
But a miller us'd him worst of all,
For he crushed him between two stones.

And they had taen his very heart's blood,
And drank it round and round;
And still the more and more they drank,
Their joy did more abound.

John Barleycorn was a hero bold,
Of noble enterprise,
For if you do but taste his blood,
'Twill make your courage rise.

'Twill make a man forget his woe;
'Twill heighten all his joy;
'Twill make the widow's heart to sing,
Tho' the tear were in her eye.

Then let us toast John Barleycorn
Each man a glass in hand;
And may his great posterity
Ne'er fail in old Scotland.

Robert Burns' associations with alcoholic drink were diverse and sometimes conflicting, as will become clear in due course.

A very important part of the laboratory work was the microbiological tests. These were carried out to ensure that no beer spoilage organisms were allowed to enter the process, either from the raw materials or through poor cleaning practices. Swabs were regularly taken of the plant after cleaning and these, together with samples of beer and raw materials, were plated out on nutrient agar plates and incubated. Within a few days, a single bacterium or wild yeast cell would grow into a visible colony which then could be counted.

Around the brewery, beer spoilage organisms, which could be acid-producing bacteria or Eric Wiles' wild yeast, were commonly referred to as 'bugs'. On one occasion the fermenting-room foreman, Joe Justice, called me to one side and asked me, partly tongue-in-cheek:

'Eh Frank, what do these bugs look like? If I see one, I'll 'it it wi't broom 'andle!'

He had clearly been 'spoken to' by the Head Brewer, Harold Burkinshaw, about a less than perfect plate count of plant within his responsibility.

In those days, Head Brewers were powerful men. Not only did

Left: Frank Priestley examining yeast under a microscope to check for the presence of beer spoilage organisms.
Right: Setting up the original gravity apparatus.

they rule the brewery with a rod of iron, but they maintained their control over the product right up until the point of sale. After all, even a perfect beer can be ruined by dirty pipes in the pub or a greasy glass. (It is believed that in ancient Babylon, when an unsatisfactory brew was encountered, it was not unheard of for the brewer to be drowned in his substandard product! I am relieved to report that more enlightened quality control measures are employed these days.)

The previous Head Brewer, Mr Jolliffe, had retired many years before I joined the company but he was still remembered for his strictness. It is said he was walking through the fermenting rooms one day when he peered over the top of an open copper vessel to inspect the cleaning. Two men were working away with brushes – it was the accepted standard that the copper would be cleaned until it shone like new. Mr Jolliffe noticed a blemish and pointed it out to the men. One of them started to explain that it was just a sun beam coming from one of the ventilation grills, but the head brewer was having none of it.

'You're not to come out of there until it's gone!'

Presumably they remained in the vessel until the sun moved round.

Without a doubt, the most pleasant duty I had as laboratory assistant was my daily visit to the sample room. It was a tunnel-shaped room with an arched ceiling and was always kept locked. It was located in the depths of the cellars and, as a result, its temperature remained constant at between 58-59 degrees F, whatever season of the year it was. This was considered the ideal temperature to taste (and drink) draught beer.

The purpose of my visits was to take samples of the beer that had been racked (filled into casks) the previous day and set them up on a gantry to settle out. By the time I took the samples, they were completely clear or bright and in perfect condition. It was extremely tempting to take a drink and invariably, I succumbed to temptation, filled a glass (of Queen's Ale, if possible) and enjoyed a few minutes of ecstasy in that little haven of peace.

The sample beers had been filled into 18 gallon casks – I had to learn quickly not to call them barrels. The word 'barrel' indicated a capacity of 36 gallons. The 18 gallon casks (half a barrel) were called Kilderkins, from the Dutch for child. 9 gallon casks (quarter of a barrel) were called Firkins, from the Dutch for fourth (just to clear up any possible misunderstanding). Hogsheads were 54 gallon casks (one and a half barrels) and pins were four and a half gallon casks (an eighth of a barrel). There were other sizes in existence but the ones above were those regularly used at Tennant's.

All down one side of the sample room were pins of Gold Label Barley Wine, stacked three or four high. Gold Label had been developed by Tennant's in 1951. It was a pale-coloured sparkling barley wine of great strength. It contained 10.6% alcohol by volume and as such was the strongest regularly brewed, nationally distributed beer in Britain.

In order to brew a beer of such strength, it was necessary to boil the wort (beer, prior to fermentation) for between two and three times longer than would be the case for an ordinary beer. The result of this prolonged boiling was to darken the beer considerably. Thus all other barley wines at that time were dark beers. The paleness of Gold Label was achieved by selecting ingredients, not only of the highest quality, but also choosing those which contributed least to the final colour – e.g. very pale malts, cereals and sugar. The sparkling effect was achieved by giving the beer a higher level of carbonation prior to bottling.

After the Gold Label had finished fermenting, it was racked into hogsheads and rolled 'up the tunnel'. This tunnel ran underneath Bridge Street and led to the cellars of an old building across the road from the brewery. I discovered later that these old cellars had previously been part of Duncan Gilmore's, the brewery that had once owned the *Banner Cross Hotel*. Gilmore's had been established in 1831 but had been taken over, and presumably closed down, by Joshua Tetley & Son of Leeds in 1954. The barley wine was held here to mature for between six months and one year. From each brew, a pin was filled and these were the casks that were stacked along one wall of the sample room. The head Brewer would regularly sample them in order to select a blend for bottling.

I also got into the habit of tasting them to round off my sampling of the draught beer. By choosing a suitably old one, I would find myself with a glass of perfectly matured barley wine. The drinking experience was incredible. The smooth malty, hoppy flavour was wonderful and as it went down, you could feel the warm alcoholic glow diffuse throughout your body. However, when there was still work to be done, it had to be treated with respect. The advice often directed at other drinks, was more than relevant here:

'A glass of barley wine is like a woman's breast – one is rarely enough, but three is one too many.'

One day I learned that the head brewer had long since banned anyone else from sampling from these casks as he had come upon one which had been drunk dry. The only other people who had access to the sample room were the brewers and although I knew that they all were partial to Gold Label, one of them in particular was suspected. This was Tom Newton, whom Tennant's had inherited when the Nottingham brewery was taken over. Tom was a large, jolly man who still wore the traditional brown brewers' boots. Whenever he saw me around the brewery, he would call out: 'Keep your bowels open laddie and trust in the Lord.' But since I was, by now, embracing the art of drinking with some enthusiasm, the first part of the advice, at least, was superfluous.

The idea of brewing a beer so strong that it could be safely stored in the cellars for many months was not new. In the past, some breweries used to stock up their cellars with such ales for use in mid-winter. Ordinary draught beers are best drunk soon after racking and should preferably be consumed within a week of tapping. During hard winters, it was sometimes impossible to ferment beers at all if breweries had insufficient means of heating their rooms. (Fermentation usually takes place around 60 – 70 degrees F.) When this happened, the trade would be supplied with the strong ale from stock. This was called 'Old Ale'.

When I was a child, my grandfather, who was born and raised in the county of Salop, sometimes used to say – 'there's old in four-penny', which seemed to mean that people had hidden depths. I have since learned the four-penny referred to the cheap mild ale that was served in public bars because the price charged was four pence a quart. In some areas, it was said that the public bar was known, for this reason, as the four-ale bar (although I am inclined to believe that it was the best bar that was so named, because it offered the full range of draught beers – four ales). If they could afford it, customers would improve their drink by mixing half a pint of mild with half a pint of old ale. Thus – old in four-penny.

The tradition of old ale is still kept alive today by a few breweries that produce it mostly for bottling. In my neck of the woods, I am able to get hold of Robinson's Old Tom and Marston's Owd Rodger – both lovely ales, and Banks's Barley Gold has a reassuringly familiar flavour to it.

The problem of not being able to maintain production throughout the year was not confined to breweries. Whisky distilleries needed constant supplies of cold water to cool the product of their distillation. This is why distilleries were traditionally sited alongside streams or rivers. If there was a dry spell in the summer, which must happen sometimes, even in Scotland and Ireland, the distillery would have to close down. This period was known as the 'silent season'.

3

Whitbread & Co Ltd

In 1962, three years after I had joined the brewery, an announcement was made to the staff and the workforce, that Tennant Brothers had merged with Whitbread & Co Ltd. 'for their mutual benefit.'

This took everyone by complete surprise. We didn't know very much about Whitbread's except that they were a large, London-based company that produced Mackeson Stout which was advertised regularly on television and Whitbread Tankard which was an early keg beer. Keg beer, unlike traditional draught, was filtered and carbonated, rather like most bottled beers. The advantage of this was that it was much more stable than draught and it remained in good condition for much longer. The disadvantages were that filtration removed some of the finer flavours and carbonation rendered it somewhat gassy to the palate of those more accustomed to traditionally conditioned ales. However, we were assured that our traditional methods and products would be retained and that we would continue to trade under the name of Tennant Brothers Ltd.

It was subsequently explained that a major incentive for the merger had been a need for Tennant's to avoid the attentions of asset strippers. At that time, there were unscrupulous speculators who were seeking out, buying up and closing down small-to-medium sized breweries in order to sell off their considerable assets. The breweries usually occupied prime sites in towns and cities and were filled with valuable copper metal. They owned hundreds of public houses: many of these also on prime sites, and very often they owned houses, rented out to their workers. When all these assets were realised, it was plain that a brewery was worth much more closed down and sold off than it was when it was purchased as a going concern.

By merging with a national company, Tennant's had evaded the grasp of the speculators. Most of us believed that this was a price well worth paying. After all, long term job security was an asset beyond price.

Gradually, over the next few years, changes were introduced. Most of Tennant's bottled beers disappeared. No. 1 Barley wine had already been swallowed up by Gold Label and then Don Jon, Lion Brown Ale and the prize-winning Lion Pale Ale were discontinued. Whitbread Pale Ale was tankered up from London and bottled in Sheffield. Glucose Stout was replaced by Mackeson which was now brewed and bottled in Sheffield. There was even a suggestion that Tennant's Gold Label should be replaced by Whitbread's barley wine, Final Selection. I believe it was due only to the persistence of our strong-willed Head Brewer, Harold Burkinshaw, that this wonderful product was saved.

Tennant's draught beers didn't fare much better. The beautiful Queen's Ale was discontinued, as was Rock Ale, which was replaced by Whitbread Best Mild. Best Bitter, after a colour adjustment, was renamed Trophy Bitter. Whitbread's policy was to advertise nation-ally a product that was, in effect, each region's Best Bitter. It was a good idea. A national product, brewed to satisfy local tastes. Although, when Yorkshiremen went on holiday down south, they sometimes got a bit of a surprise when they ordered their favourite brew.

Nor did Tennant's name remain sacrosanct for long. Whitbread's had acquired two more breweries in the West Riding – Kirkstall Brewery at Leeds and Bentley's Yorkshire Brewery at nearby Woodlesford. The three were clumped together as 'Whitbread Yorkshire' and Tennant Brothers Ltd., which was designated the regional head quarters, became known as, 'Whitbread Yorkshire – Sheffield'. Later on, two more sites were included – the distribution depot at Loughborough and Nimmo's Brewery in Co. Durham and the region became known as 'Whitbread East Pennines'. The merger was beginning to feel like a take-over.

On the other hand, being part of a national group had many positive aspects – not least, the improved career opportunities available to keen young beer enthusiasts such as myself. When I had first started at the brewery, the position of laboratory assistant had been vacant because the previous post holder, Peter Shepherd, had been promoted and put in charge of a small laboratory in the bottling hall. Now, under Whitbread's, Peter was given the opportunity to train as a bottling supervisor, the first rung of the middle management ladder, while I took his place in the bottling laboratory.

By this time, we were bottling many national products such as Whitbread Pale Ale and Forest Brown, Mackeson and of course Gold Label. The additional methods and procedures that this involved and which had opened the door for Peter to join the expanding management team had also increased the workload in the laboratory and consequently, I was given a female assistant. This was a new experience for me. I remember one day accidentally walking into one of the gas taps that extended from the sides of the work benches. I hurt myself in a way that only a man could understand.

'Are you alright?' asked Susan, sweetly.

'Er, yes. I've only injured my pride.'

The range of work carried out in the bottling laboratory was not as great as that in the brewery but there were some new and interesting procedures to learn. All bottled beers were tested for carbon dioxide levels and haze and we had a new piece of apparatus to measure the air content of beer in bottle. A significant level of air in beer can encourage haziness and flavour deterioration. It was important then, to keep this to the absolute minimum.

This was achieved by the use of a neat piece of equipment on the bottling line. After each bottle had been filled, a device known as the 'knocker', tapped the side of the bottle, causing it to froth up. The process was timed so that the bottle was capped just as the froth reached the neck, thus expelling virtually all of the air. At least, that was the theory. You can imagine the 'fun' the operatives had trying to make it work, bearing in mind that different beers had different levels of carbonation and that beer bottles (which were still returnable) were by no means uniform.

Samples were taken throughout the processing and bottling stages for microbiological testing. Processing beer prior to bottling consisted of cooling it down to around 33 degrees F (beer freezes at a lower temperature than water) and then carbonating and filtering it. The beer needed to be so cold because firstly, carbon dioxide is more soluble at lower temperatures and secondly, the filtration process would remove not only any trace of yeast present but also protein which would fall out of solution at this temperature.

The tank rooms where the beer was stored were necessarily very cold, and a shock to the system if you had just walked in from the steamy, warm bottling hall. The number of times I stepped into this arctic environment muttering:

'God, it's cold in here!' only to hear the reply, 'I've known it colder.'

This came from ex-Royal Marine, Ernest Oxley who was one of the cold room chargehands. During the Second World War, one of the places he'd served was on the North Sea convoys to Murmansk in Russia. They actually docked at Polyarnyy, which they renamed 'Polly Annie'. He used to take pleasure in telling me that if you spat, it would freeze before it hit the deck. I once made the mistake of calling him a marine. '*Royal* Marine! You bum!' I considered his rebuke well deserved.

The operatives on the bottling line were female – many of them young girls who had the reputation for working hard and playing hard. When I first started in the department, every time I went to fetch some bottles off the line for sampling, one particular girl used to try, and used to succeed, in embarrassing me. She was a slim, dark haired girl and as I approached, she used to squeal and whistle in order to draw everyone's attention to me. One day, one of the older women said to me, 'Why don't you tell her to bollocks?' So I did. Everyone laughed, including me. After that, it became a game. Every time I went out onto the line, she'd squeal, I'd shout 'Bollocks', and everybody would laugh. I was no longer embarrassed. I believed that I was beginning to understand the complexities of the female psyche.

Most of the girls wore wooden clogs, which was just as well – the floor was covered with broken glass. However, they were always reluctant to wear the protective glasses that they'd been given, in spite of the fact that faulty bottles frequently exploded on the filling machine, flinging splinters of glass in all directions. They wore white overalls which were laundered at the end of each week. It was up to each individual to mark theirs so that they got the correct one back. I remember one good-looking blonde haired girl who had the word PAT written across the left breast of her overall. I am ashamed to admit that, at that stage in my life, I was still too bashful to avail myself of her generous invitation.

On the last working day before Christmas, we had a 'slightly' extended lunch break and we'd all pile into the *Lady's Bridge Hotel*, the pub next to the brewery. The combination of alcohol, jukebox and fun-loving girls made for memorable experiences, the recollection of which I still cherish today, but which discretion dissuades me from describing. Later on, I'd sneak back to the lab and try to appear sober.

Around this time, a new tank room was built which could be reached from the bottling hall, via a bridge across Mill Sands, the lane at the side of the brewery. The new room housed a large number of 200 barrel tanks. They were used for the maturation of Gold Label. The practice of maturing 'in wood', up the tunnel, had been discontinued. Not only that, but the maturation time was progressively reduced. So much for the retention of traditional methods, I thought. However, to be fair, the sales of Gold Label were rising phenomenally and from the volume alone, it would have been very difficult to mature the product in the old way. A newly-designed bottle label, carrying the Whitbread name, was brought in to replace the Tennant's label. This was fair enough: after all, it was no longer Tennant's Gold Label.

The first bottling manager that I knew was Geoff Brown – one of life's true gentlemen. His office was up a flight of stairs, overlooking the whole bottling area. Adjoining his office was a small, discrete room which became an unofficial haven for staff who were harassed or thirsty or both. Geoff kept it well stocked with Gold Label 'shorts'. These were bottles that were slightly under filled, usually through overflowing at the 'knocker'. In theory, they should have been decanted individually into casks and then blown back into a tank. This was clearly time-consuming and labour intensive. It was obviously less trouble to drink them. The room was known as 'Brown's Bar' and was often patronised by brewers.

On one occasion, a brewer, seeking to evade the scrutiny of the head brewer, made his way down to Brown's Bar for a quick break and a 'snifter'. His colleague, who was holding the fort in the brewery, caught sight of the head brewer striding swiftly towards the bottling department. The fort-holding colleague rushed back to the brewing office to phone a warning to his friend.

'H.B. is on his way down!' To which came the rather cold reply,

'This is H.B. speaking.'

A later manager was more of the pre-war vintage and so was his suit. The jacket had long, pointed lapels, slightly curved outwards and the generously wide trousers were suspended from a pair of ancient bracers. When he was surveying his domain from the elevated office, he had the habit of toying with his left bracer clip, stretching the strap like a chest expander. The result of this activity was that when he later went down to inspect the line, while his right trouser bottom was flapping around his shoes, his left one was hoisted a good four inches above his ankle. Consequently, the girls gave him the otherwise inexplicable nick-name of 'Odd-legs'.

Another manager, who hailed from the London area, was

known as 'Swim'. This was because he suffixed every instruction he gave, with the phrase, '*see what I mean?*'

Under Whitbread's, there were several bottling managers but the little room behind the office was always known as Brown's Bar.

4

The Tower

I had been working in the laboratories now for seven years and was beginning to feel that I would like to move on to something more challenging. It was timely then, when Peter Shepherd brought me some interesting news. He had heard that the company was looking for someone to train as a supervisor in the brewery. He was keen to pursue his career in packaging and so was not interested but he wondered if perhaps I was. It was just the right opportunity at the right time and I was, and remain, eternally grateful to Peter for putting it my way. When I spoke to the Chief Chemist, he said that he didn't realise that I might be interested as I had always seemed so happy in the bottling department. Mind you, surrounded by Gold Label and girls, who would not seem happy?

I was duly accepted for the training and Ronnie Lumb, the Second Brewer, worked out a programme for me. Normally, it would take twelve months but since I was already fairly familiar with the brewery and the brewing process, this was reduced to six months. The training involved working alongside the men in each department for one week on each shift. It had always been the case that the management in breweries (that is, brewers) would never ask a man to do a task that he was not capable of carrying out himself. In the days before academic qualifications had been established, young men wishing to become brewers would seek to serve a pupilage with an established brewer. This would involve working on the shop floor for a year or more. It seemed as though a similar principle was being applied to me.

It was decided that I would start my training at the beginning of the brewing process and work my way progressively to the finished product. The brewery had originally been built using the 'tower system'. That is, the main part of the brewery consisted of a tower block in which the process began on the top floor. Motivated by gravity, each successive stage took the beer a floor lower until the finished product was racked into casks on the cellar floor. This energy-efficient system was commonly employed in breweries built in Victorian times.

Over the years, the Sheffield brewery had been modified by the introduction of a few pumps and conveyors, but it still remained essentially a tower. In consequence, my training began on the roof, where the liquor tanks were located and in the subsequent months, it would be possible to measure my progress by taking note of what altitude I was working at.

The first task that I learned was the treatment of brewing liquor. The salts were dissolved in a small vessel and then injected into the huge liquor tanks, known as 'pans'. These were heated up during the night, ready for the next day's brewing. Mackeson, being mild flavoured, needed less treatment than the draught beers and full bodied Gold Label needed the most treatment of all.

Sacks of malt were hoisted from the maltsters' lorries in the yard, up to the malt room. Each sack contained one quarter (336 lbs) of malt. In those days, malt was made from varieties of barley with names like Plumage, Proctor and Earl. The names of the maltsters were written on the sacks but you could tell what kind of malt it was from the colour of the string used to tie up the neck of the sack. Dark malts were used in the brewing of stout and also to darken beers. They were produced by giving the barley an extra roasting at certain stages in the malting process. They had names such as Brown, Crystal and Chocolate. The brewers supplied the malt room with a 'grist ticket' for each brew. This told the men how

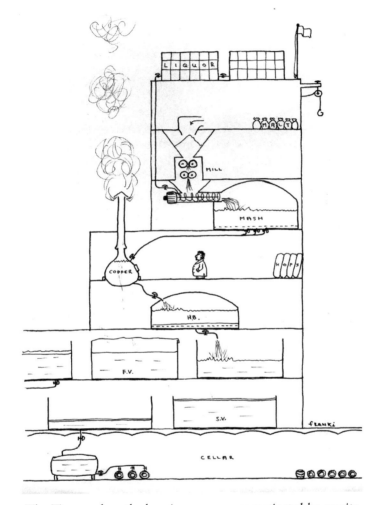

The Tower, where the brewing process was motivated by gravity.

many sacks of each variety were required. The malt was tipped into a hopper, which led to the mill room.

The mill had two sets of rollers, the first just to crack the malt, the second to grind it. It was a surprisingly dangerous procedure. There were occasionally small pieces of metal mixed in with the malt, probably from farm machinery. If such a piece made contact with the hard steel rollers, a spark could be produced which would ignite the fine, dry dust which accompanied the malt, causing the mill to explode. Consequently, a strong magnet was placed in the flow of the malt prior to milling. The ground up malt or grist fell into the grist case, a large hopper, feeding the mashing machine.

The mashing process was really the heart of the brew house. It was here that hot liquor was mixed with grist at a rate of two barrels per quarter, which gave it the consistency of porridge. The purpose of the mash was to allow the enzymes in the malt to convert its starchy contents into malt sugar. The temperature of the mash was extremely critical. A change of just five degrees F could make the difference between a full-bodied beer suitable for storing and a readily-fermentable beer intended for quick consumption. In the days before thermometers, it is said that brewers checked the heat of the mash by sticking their thumbs in it, thus giving rise to the expression, 'rule of thumb'.

Other expressions that have entered the language from brewing, are 'scraping the barrel' and 'brewers' droop', although concerning the latter I have never known a drinking man, brewer or not, admit to suffering from this unfortunate condition. I'm sure it must be a myth. What is not a myth however, is that many a man, 'in his cups', has had his tongue twisted into the sort of Spoonerism such as 'drewers' broop'. I personally have been known to refer to Ronnie Lumb, the Second Brewer as Lonnie Rum and to Charlie Binns, the esteemed Chief Engineer as Barley Chins. (Decency prevents me from articulating the Spoonerism that has been unkindly applied to Whitbread Tankard.)

The mash was contained in a large, shallow, cylindrical vessel with a perforated false bottom, called the mash tun. After standing for one and a half hours, the conversion to malt sugar was complete and the taps were opened at the bottom. On a cold morning, (the first mash started at five a.m.) there was nothing so warming and nourishing as a mug of hot malt extract, taken straight from the taps. This was sometimes known as the 'brewer's breakfast'. As the extract flowed down to the coppers, hot liquor was sprinkled on top of the mash, leaching through the grain. This was called sparging. When everything had been extracted from the mash, just the spent grains were left. They were heavy and steaming hot but needed to be moved in time for the next brew.

When I first started at the brewery, it was necessary for a man to climb into the mash tun and shovel the grains out of the plug hole. The heat and steam made it an exhausting job and for this, the man received 'grains allowance', which consisted of a couple of pints of beer. This was in addition to the standard beer allowance that all the brewery workers received, which was a pint at morning break and another in the afternoon.

During my time in the bottling department, a rotary arm had been fitted into the mash tun, which removed most of the grains mechanically so that the man only had to jump in at the end to sweep out the last few handfuls. Nevertheless, he still received the full grains allowance. I think that it was highly commendable that the man insisted on preserving the old traditions.

The coppers were onion-shaped copper vessels where the wort, as it was called, was boiled. The word 'wort' usually referred to any kind of plant used as a herb and it is thought that brewers' wort got its name because the unfermented beer was spiced up with herbs at this stage. Before the almost universal use of hops, other herbs, such as wormwood and alehoof were used. In those distant days, the Scots, never being ones to miss out on a plentiful and therefore cheap resource, used to flavour their ale with heather. I believe that this tradition has now been restored by a brewer in Strathaven.

The hops were delivered to the brewery in enormous sacks,

known ironically as 'pockets'. There were two main varieties, Goldings and Fuggles. Goldings was a variety which had been discovered by a Mr Golding, a Kentish hop grower, growing in his garden in the Malling district towards the end of the 18th century. He described it as 'a plant of extraordinary quality and productiveness.' He proceeded to distribute cuttings to his neighbours and the variety gradually spread throughout East Kent. Fuggles originated in 1861 from a seed which was thrown out with some crumbs on the farm of Mr George Stace of Horsmonden, Kent. The resulting plant was subsequently introduced to commerce by Mr Richard Fuggle of Brenchley around 1871.

Hops were unusual in that they had separate male and female plants. A hop cone was the fertilised female flower and as such, contained seeds. Continental hop growers did not like seeds in their hops and to achieve this, they deprived their female plants of the attention of the males. It was illegal to allow a male plant to grow anywhere near a hop field. Understandably perhaps, the female continental hop cones were more 'bitter'. Even so, I believe that the English hops had a delicacy of flavour and aroma that could not be matched anywhere.

The wort in the coppers was brought up to the boil and the hops were added. The soft resins in the hops imparted their bitter flavour to the beer but unfortunately the volatile oils, which were responsible for the hop's fine aroma, were largely boiled out of the copper chimney with the steam. This loss was remedied later by adding half an ounce per barrel of hops to the finished beer as it was racked into casks. This was known as 'dry hopping' and it ensured that the beer retained the precious aroma of English hops.

A good vigorous boil in the coppers was essential, not only to extract the bitterness from the hops, but also to get a good separation of unwanted protein, a process which was greatly assisted by the presence of hop tannins. It was necessary to drive off enough steam to get the wort to the required strength and liquid sugar could be added at this stage to contribute to the final strength

The onion-shaped no.5 copper vessel at Sheffield, where the 'wort' was brought to the boil so as to separate any unwanted protein and kill any beer spoilage organisms.

of the beer. Finally, a good boil would ensure that the wort was sterilised and free from any beer spoilage organisms.

After the boil was complete, the wort was run down to the 'hopback'. This was a generous vessel with a perforated false bottom and consequently, it looked rather like a large mash tun. The wort stood for half an hour in the hopback and during that time, the hops and coagulated protein matter settled on the false bottom to form a filter bed. When the wort was subsequently pumped from the bottom of the vessel into the fermenting rooms, it was filtered clear and bright. Before it reached the fermenting vessels, the wort was run through a heat exchanger which cooled it down to around 60 degrees F and as it ran into the vessels, yeast was added at the rate of one pound per barrel.

Yeast is a primitive single-celled fungus and, unlike green plants, it cannot synthesise its own food. It gains its energy by breaking down sugars and produces carbon dioxide and alcohol as by-products. It is highly ironical then that this, one of the lowest forms of life, facilitates one of the most wonderful inventions of man.

As the fermentation proceeded, the temperature of the beer rose. This heat was the result of an orgy of passion as the yeast reproduced to four or five times its original weight in the space of a couple of days or so. As the sugars were broken down to alcohol, the gravity of the beer progressively fell and when it was down to the required level, the riot of reproduction was finally brought to an end by slowly cooling the beer down to 53 degrees F and by removing most of the yeast crop.

The original method for removing yeast in Tennant's days was the Dropping System. Beer was fermented in open, circular, copper vessels filled to about two-thirds their capacity in order to leave space for the large yeast head that was produced. At the end of fermentation, the beer was run or 'dropped' into a copper settling vessel where it was cooled down. These vessels were situated on the floor immediately below the fermenting rooms. The settling vessels did not need to be as large as the fermenting vessels since they did not need to accommodate the yeast head which was left behind in the fermenting vessel and later recovered via the plug hole. One of the advantages of this system was that the fermenting vessels could be filled twice a week instead of only once.

In the 1950s, Tennant's had installed some modern (for that time) stainless steel, open, square fermenting vessels, alongside the old copper ones. These new vessels had no settling vessels beneath them and consequently, the beer remained in them for a whole week – heating up during fermentation and cooling down thereafter. By this time, yeast removal from both copper and stainless steel vessels was implemented by sucking the yeast through a nozzle, from the top of the beer into a tank which had been kept under partial vacuum. The yeast could then be blown to one of the yeast rooms. A small amount of yeast, about one inch thick, was left on top of the body of the beer to protect it from air-borne spoilage organisms.

Although all the beers tasted fine to the general drinker, it was possible for a trained taster, such as myself in the sample room, to detect slight differences in the beers from different vessels. During fermentation, yeast produced traces of sulphury compounds which were rather harsh to the taste. These compounds reacted with brightly cleaned copper and were thus removed from the beer. In steel vessels, no such reaction took place, so although these vessels were easier to clean, they did not produce as good a flavour as the copper ones. I found that the best flavour of all was produced by fermenting in a copper fermenting vessel and dropping into a copper settling vessel.

Because the yeast reproduced so enthusiastically, we always finished up with much more than we needed. The best of the crop was directed into a yeast room which was kept, as near as possible, in a sterile state and this yeast was used for future brews. The remainder, which was considerable, was diverted to an old yeast room in an area of the cellars known as the Barm Alley. When the yeast arrived here, it was in the form of a slurry. It was blown through a filter press which held the yeast back and the beer which had been mixed with the yeast (known as pressings) was returned to the fermenting vessels. The dried yeast was packed into old casks and sold to the food industry.

The charge hand in the Barm Alley was Jock McKinnon. He was a remarkable man and, not surprisingly, Scottish. I discovered that he used to drink Gold Label pressings. This was basically Gold Label with a very harsh, yeasty flavour. From my time working in that department, I learned that it was quite possible to get used to drinking this foul dose. There was clearly no pleasure in the drinking of it, it was more like taking a medicine – you put up with the taste knowing that you were going to feel very much better, very quickly. Jock used to mask the smell of it on his breath by the liberal use of mouthwash from the first aid box in the department.

You could always tell how much Jock had had to drink in the course of the day. He wore a cap at work and first thing in the morning, the peak was centrally aligned above the front of his face, like that of the guardsman he once was. As the day wore on and his sobriety became eroded, the peak would progressively move round his head, like the shadow on a sun dial.

Kind friends have pointed out that I also demonstrate a similar 'alcohol barometer' when drinking barley wines. As I lift the glass to my lips, my elbow becomes somewhat elevated and the more glasses that I have consumed, the greater the angle of elevation. I consider that this is a rather refined and superior reaction to alcohol. It could be a lot worse.

Some people talk loudly when 'in drink', while others become silent. Others become violent, while some fall over without the aid of violence. Some become depressed, while others become elated and some become ill while others lose interest and consciousness. In addition to my elevated elbow, my own emotional reaction to alcohol is that I become amorous. Believe me: this can cause just as many problems as any of the other reactions.

The next department that I worked in was the cask washing shed where empty casks were washed out prior to filling. The casks were rolled over a series of jets which flushed them out with hot water and steam. Working in this department was another Scotsman also called Jock. He was an elderly man and he was known as 'Wee Jock'. This was to distinguish him from the other Jock and also because he was small of stature. His accent was so broad that no-one could understand a word he said. It was believed that originally he came from Glasgow.

An occasion arose when the brewery football team was scheduled to play a team from Whitbread Scotland in Glasgow. Many of us, including Wee Jock, went up to Scotland with the team to support them. The strange thing was that even the people in Glasgow could not understand Wee Jock. It was one of those mysteries that breweries seem prone to.

In the cellar, the beer was run down from the settling or fermenting vessels and filled into casks and dry hopped. This took place in a relatively small area. The remainder of the cellars, which were quite extensive, was used to store the casks of beer until they were required for the trade.

A hogshead of beer weighed about a quarter of a ton and that was not including the substantial weight of the oak cask. And yet a man of average physique could transport this leviathan across the cellar floor with just an occasional push from the palms of his hands and could bring it to a halt by tapping the end of the cask with his foot, setting it spinning on its 'hump'. Of course, I'm talking about an experienced man here. It was painful (for all concerned) to watch a novice making his debut on the cellar floor. If he was not risking back strain or a hernia, he was getting his fingers crushed between one cask and another or between a cask and the wall.

The cellar was an important department for all those who worked in the brewery, for it was here that the beer allowance was issued. Men came down at the allotted time and filled their glasses, jugs, cans or whatever from a tap in the wall. Some drank it there and then, sitting on the benches provided. Others took it back to be enjoyed in the warmth of their own departments. It was all supervised by the cellar foreman. A few men did not take any allowance; they preferred a can of tea, while others somehow managed to scrounge an extra pint. I took the view that a man doing heavy physical work would soon assimilate a few pints. During my time in the Sheffield brewery, there was quite a turnover of cellar foremen. Some people became superstitious about it, particularly as they all had names beginning with the letter 'H' – Arthur Hunter, Eddie Hardy, Bill Hopkinson and Brian Helliwell.

When beer was required for the trade, it was rolled up onto the loading stage. Here it was primed and fined at the rate of four pints of finings and three pints of primings per barrel. Finings was made out of isinglass and this helped the remaining yeast to settle out to give a clear bright beer. Primings was a sugar solution which enabled the yeast to continue fermenting and this maintained the level of carbonation of the beer. The rolling about and moving on and off the lorry ensured that everything was well mixed in by the time the cask reached the cellar of the public house. After 'setting up' on the gantry, it would be in perfect condition within 24 hours.

These days, it annoys me more than I can say; when I am served a flat, cloudy pint and the bar staff justifies this by saying that it's *real* ale. Traditional cask conditioned beer should be as clear as crystal and sparkling with bubbles which form a thick, creamy head that rolls over the side of the glass – and nothing less.

The charge hand on the loading stage was Bernard Smith, an Irishman from Dublin. In comparisons between the English and the Irish, it is sometimes said – 'To the English, things are often serious, but never disastrous, but to the Irish, things are often disastrous but never serious.' Nothing was serious to Bernard. He took everything in his stride. When the pressure was on and beer orders were coming in thick and fast, he would simply smile and say, 'When the good Lord made time, He made plenty of it.'

He once told me a story of his early days in Dublin. He had been drinking in a bar near the old Guinness Brewery. The evening was late, the bar was full and the atmosphere was congenial. Suddenly, a stranger burst in through the door. With his hands thrust deep in his pockets, he was dancing what looked like a jig. His face was constantly changing expression and he was not so much singing as uttering a series of short cries in time with his disjointed dance. The customers could not decide whether he was 'a bit simple' or just plain drunk.

In any event, they clapped him and cheered, just to give him some encouragement. It was not until he fell to the floor that they realised that the man was in some pain. An ambulance was sent for and he was taken to the hospital. Later, they learned the truth of the matter. He had been walking along a near-by street when a rat had run from a partly demolished building and bumped into his foot in the dark. It had run up his trouser leg and sunk its teeth into his private parts, or at least one of them. And it was in that awful condition, that he had staggered into the bar for help.

'Was he alright?' I asked, in some alarm.

'Oh yes,' answered Bernard, 'but the rat was never the same again!'

On another occasion, the cellar foreman came up onto the loading stage wearing his newly-issued overall. It was a brown warehouse coat which would normally reach down to his knees. But because considerable shrinkage took place the first time the overalls were sent to the laundry, new ones were always ordered several sizes too large, to compensate for this. The overall the foreman was wearing almost reached his shoes and he felt very self-conscious about it.

'Don't worry', said Bernard cheerfully, 'it suits you down to the ground.'

'It fits me down to the bloody ground,' answered the foreman, without humour.

The next department was the cooperage and although I worked there for a week, taking great pleasure in what I saw, this was one department in the brewery where no-one would tell the men how to do their work. A cooper was a craftsman in his own right, with techniques and skills that could be traced back to 2,690 BC on ancient Egyptian tomb paintings. Consequently, it would be presumptuous of me to attempt to describe what a cooper did.

Our head cooper was Les Wallace and the other coopers were Jim Walker and Eric Cooper (appropriate name). It took five years to train as a cooper – a good indication of the skills involved. At the end of the apprenticeship, the traditional ceremony of 'trussing-in' was carried out. The newly trained cooper was rolled around the brewery yard in a hogshead into which all sorts of rubbish had been poured – stale, yeasty beer collected from returned casks plus sawdust and wood shavings and anything else that could be swept off the floor of the cooperage. It was not a day to be forgotten.

The coopers made their casks out of memel oak, grown in the Baltic district and these could last for thirty years or more. Even if they became damaged by being clumsily handled off the back of a lorry, a split stave could soon be replaced back in the cooperage.

The cooper's yard at Sheffield, full of the wooden casks made out of memel oak.

Besides being a remarkably mobile container, as described earlier, wooden casks had another important advantage. Metal casks were beginning to appear on the scene at this time as they were relatively cheap. But the beer in one of these, sitting on the back of a lorry, would quickly overheat in summer or become chilled in winter causing problems with condition and clarity. Wood, being a good insulator, prevented this situation from arising.

It is a testimony to the strength and versatility of these containers that Carlisle Graham, an English cooper, was the first person to ride the Niagara Rapids and over the Falls in 1886. His vessel was an oak cask which had been constructed to such dimensions as would accommodate the human form. Surprisingly, he repeated this feat on several occasions.

With the continued increase in the use of metal casks (two apertures), kegs (one aperture) and tank beer, there has been a drastic decline in the number of coopers working in breweries. At the time of writing, there is only a handful left. It would be a tragedy if these skills and traditions, not to mention these unique containers, disappeared forever.

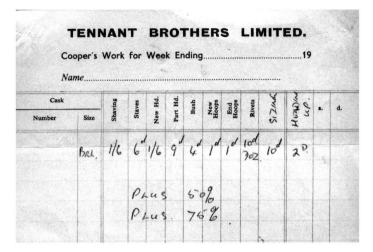

The cooper's worksheet.

I am reminded of a few lines from the song, *The Rare Ould Times.*

My name it is Sean Dempsey
As Dublin as could be,
Born hard and late in Pimlico
In a house that's ceased to be.
By trade I am a cooper
Lost out to redundancy,
Like my house that fell to progress
My trade's a memory.

© by Celtic Songs/Emma Music Ltd. Used by permission of the Valentine Music Group, London

For several weeks, I worked in the engineers department, studying the refrigeration plant, the boiler house and the power supply. The technology involved in these was only the same as you would find in any numbers of industries and as such, does not deserve a mention here. What does deserve mention however, is that the engineers were the unsung heroes of the brewery. Most traditional breweries had been built in Victorian times or before but they were now working to the commercial and production standards of the second half of the 20th century. They were museum pieces being maintained and modified by the fitters and electricians of the engineers department who rarely got a mention – except when things went wrong.

The long-suffering Chief Engineer was Charlie Binns and when he retired, his assistant Roy Allott took over. Peter Morfitt became Roy's assistant. At any one time, they were either commissioning a new piece of plant or repairing old ones. More usually, they were doing both of these things. They were invariably working under pressure. I remember one time, when some alterations were being made to the malt room, I noticed a rather unexpected hole in the malt room floor. As I was walking down to the brew house, wondering what to do about it, I spotted Peter rushing past.

'There's a hole in the malt room floor,' I called after him.

'I'll look into it,' he called back, as he disappeared into the next department.

There was also a coppersmith who worked in the brewery. His name was Charlie Spooner and he worked closely with the engineers. 'Closely' was the operative word because the brewery had long since been trying to, 'get a pint out of a half pint glass'. Space was always a scarce commodity and there were sometimes conflicts of interest. Charlie used to swear quite a lot – not in an aggressive or insulting way – it was just that every other word was a swear word. That was his way of speaking and if he encountered a particularly long word and he wasn't able to wait until the end of it before he swore, he would break the word up and insert his curse into the middle of it.

On one occasion, when he was running a new pipe across the ceiling of the filter room, he encountered some installation that the engineers had put up. Not only was it in the way of his pipeline but he had banged his head on it. He was heard to utter the classic 'Charleyism', 'Engibleedineers and eleceffingtricians!'

I also spent several weeks working with the Cellar Service department, looking at the cellars of public houses. I learned how to dismantle and clean beer engines and other dispensing equipment and, equally important, how to clean the beer pipes. It was perhaps just as well that the general public did not have access to these places. For whereas modern cellars are spacious, temperature-controlled rooms with smooth concrete floors and tiled walls, cellars from some of the older pubs left much to be desired. While the customers enjoyed their pints in oak beamed, horse brassed comfort, beneath their feet, the most important part of the house - the cellar - may well have been little more than a cramped and poorly lit cavern. It was a testimony to the publican's skill that when the number and variety of products was increasing, he was still able to serve the 'perfect pint' at the bar.

Whatever the adverse conditions, a pub cellar, at the very least, should maintain a consistent temperature, ideally 55 – 59 degrees F, it should be dry (no moulds) and it should be *clean*.

The last few weeks of my training programme were spent working alongside the shift brewers. They worked a three shift system; the early shift – 5.00 am-1.30pm, catching the first mash at 5.00am, the day shift – 8.00am-4.30pm and the late shift – 5.00pm until the last brew was safely collected in the fermenting vessel, which was usually around 1.00am-2.00am. Tom Newton, the oldest of the three brewers, was due to retire and I learned that it was his duties that I would eventually be taking over. I spent most of the time working with the two younger men – Ron Sugden, who had originally come from Clarkson's Brewery, Barnsley and Roy Linell, who had a gentle sense of humour.

Roy once told me that he and Ron used to race, against the clock, down the tower from the roof to the cellar. There was only one rule and that was that you could not use the lift. It was up to the individual to work out the fastest route – down ladders, racing across departments, down spiral staircases, down wooden stairs and stone steps, hoping against hope that you didn't meet anybody coming the other way. Roy did tell me what the impressive record was, and it was measured in mere seconds but not surprisingly, the mists of time and alcohol have erased it from my memory.

These two men patiently taught me the daily routine of their working lives, but more than that, they taught me a great deal about the art of brewing and as I got to know them better, I was pleased to be numbered amongst their many friends.

5

Strangers in Leather Trousers

By the beginning of 1967, I had started my career as a Production Supervisor, working shifts in the brewery. The job could be conveniently divided into three sections; supervision of the process, supervision of the men and record-keeping.

Supervision of the process involved scrutinising each brew from beginning to end and taking samples at various stages to check such characteristics as colour, haze, gravity, temperature and smell (or nose). The culmination of all this was the checking of the beers in the sample room. I now had to learn how to *taste* beer as opposed to drinking it. This was done on a daily basis by whichever of the brewers was available. Beers were set up on the day of racking and checked first after 24 hours. They were then checked daily for the next 14 days.

There were four aspects to examining sample room beers: clarity, nose, flavour and head. A small amount of beer was run off the cask into a bucket and then a narrow, slender sample glass was filled with fresh beer. The glass was held level with the sighting light (a bright bulb) and then lowered slightly so that the light did not dazzle but shone down at an angle to the taster's line of vision. In this way, the slightest haze in the beer could be detected. Next, the glass was raised to the nose and the aroma was drawn in with a generous sniff. Our sense of smell is many hundreds or even thousands of times more sensitive than our sense of taste and a great deal can be learned of the flavour by testing the 'nose' in this way. Finally, the beer was tasted. A generous mouthful was taken and swilled vigorously around the mouth. Different areas of the tongue are more sensitive to particular flavours, with the front of the tongue detecting sweet tastes and the back of the tongue being more sensitive to sour and bitter tastes.

The moment of truth had arrived. The beer was spit out into a conveniently located spittoon and with eyes closed; the brain concentrated and evaluated all the many and various messages being received from the straining taste buds. The taster then recorded his coded verdict in a large sample-room book which was supported

Frank with Brian Spencer, who is holding a glass to up to a sighting light in order to observe the clarity of the beer.

on a lectern worthy of any parish church. He may have also felt constrained to add further comments, as necessary, such as 'nutty', 'fruity' or 'old nose'.

It was important not to swallow any beer during a tasting session, otherwise all subsequent beers would taste like the one swallowed. An experienced taster could taste a dozen or more samples without any problems, but if the number was significantly more than this, it was usually wise to take a break or drink a mouthful of water to clean the palate. (This is the only instance in this book when I recommend the drinking of water.)

As far as head was concerned, it was easy to pour a glass of beer with a frothy head, but a good head was one that was stable and firm enough to be retained for as long as it took to finish the glass. A good indication of a stable head was when it left a lace-like pattern on the inside of the glass as the beer was drunk and made a series of descending rings on the glass, showing where each mouthful had been taken. This effect was known as 'lacing' and was much to be desired.

I now found myself with the responsibility for managing more than a hundred men. How was I going to achieve this? These were men who had known me since I had left school to work in the laboratory. More recently, I had worked alongside them on an equal footing, sharing their jokes, beer allowance and any tricks of the trade that management was not supposed to know about. I was only going to be able to manage these men if we developed mutual respect.

Most of them, particularly the foremen, were of my father's generation. They had lived through the war and many of them had served in it. They knew me as Frank and that was how it was going to stay. I believed it would have been inappropriate to ask them to call me Mr Priestley and if an extra pint of beer was consumed here or there, I was quite willing to turn a blind eye to it so long as the job was done properly. Men who enjoyed good beer would certainly take a pride in their part in producing it and there was certainly a great deal of pride in the brewery and its products. Once a man had got a job in the brewery, he rarely left. Often, they would try to get their sons and/or brothers in as well. There were several family groups working in the brewery – the Elvins, Horsefields, Bennetts, Smiths and others.

It should be clear from the above that I already had a lot of respect for the foremen and men. It now remained for me to gain their respect and for this, I would need to demonstrate fairness as a manager and skill and good judgment in the technicalities of brewing good beer.

The nerve centre of the brewery was the brewing room. In this office stood a substantial desk, the brewing desk, and on this desk lay the brewing book. This was a large book which took up most of the desk space when it was open. On each pair of facing pages were recorded all the details of each brew, including the weights of malt, cereal, sugars and hops used and the varieties used, all the temperatures, dips, gravities etc. from the mashing of the grist to the racking of the finished beer, a week later. In other words, the book contained a minute by minute record of every drop of beer that was brewed. It was important to keep it up to date at all times, not least of all because the Head Brewer was always checking it.

Not far from the brewing room was a small office that was made available for H. M. Customs and Excise. There was an Excise man permanently attached to the brewery and in those days it was Ron Weston. There was also an Excise book that I had to fill in and not only was it very complicated but it was also a legal document so that if I made a mistake or an alteration, I could be breaking the law. It was necessary to give prior notice of the amounts of materials to be used and the movement of any materials from one vessel to another.

Every single vessel in the brewery had an official number painted on it, so that for instance, the first mash tun was MT-1, fermenting vessel three was FV-3 and the second settling vessel was SB-B and so on. When I made an entry in the excise book, I had to countersign it with my signature, FVP. It was the Excise man's job to go around the brewery with his dipstick, saccharometer and thermometer and check that we were doing all that we said that we were going to do and from his figures, he calculated the burdensome duty that the brewery was compelled to pay. If he found an anomaly, he had the power to confiscate a brew. If it was a serious misrepresentation of the facts, he could close down the brewery! This had once happened to a Scottish brewery.

However, I found our own officer, Ron Weston, very helpful in explaining to me the mysteries and intricacies of the Excise book and in fact he had quite a sense of humour. On one occasion, when he had a trainee with him who had been scrutinising the Excise book for some time, Ron sent him out into the brewery to find FVP. I don't know how long the poor soul wandered and searched among the fermenting vessels before he realised that FVP was somewhat more mobile than those stately vessels.

Despite the fact that they were responsible for working out the beer duty, Excise men were generally welcome in the brewery. Ronnie Lumb, the Second Brewer, used to say that they were 'free white coats', meaning that they were unpaid members of staff whose presence afforded some degree of supervision. My own view was that the Excise man and his regulations imposed a useful discipline on the activities of brewers. In a drinking environment, the self- discipline of brewers and others might otherwise have become excessively 'relaxed'.

Ron Weston had had some experience in Scottish whisky distilleries and it was he who told me the story of *The Distillers Funeral*.

In the old days, there were many more distilleries in Scotland than there are today. It is true that most of them were small, family concerns. Nevertheless, their owners were proud of the distinctive quality of the whisky they produced. They guarded the secrets of their art jealously. Very often, the precise details of the process at each stage were confined to a few hand-picked men who were known to be trustworthy.

However, in spite of this, the distillers had a deep respect for each other, by and large. They sometimes met socially and if one of their number should pass away, they would all wish to pay their respects at his funeral.

On one such sad occasion, two of the distillers arrived at the Kirk more than an hour early. There had been some misunderstanding of the arrangements. One had come from Perth and the other had come from Glasgow. It was a bitterly cold day and so the two men decided to seek the warmth of a near-by hotel for 'a wee refreshment' until the service was due to begin.

As they approached the bar, the man from Glasgow put his hand in his pocket to buy the first round. There was a good selection of whiskies on offer, including those distilled by the two men themselves. He pondered which he should choose. He did not wish to be seen enjoying a competitor's wares but on the other hand, he did not wish to offend his colleague.

'Which brand shall we drink?' he asked.

'I think we should drink your brand, if you don't mind,' answered the man from Perth.

They spent a pleasant hour, reminiscing and warming themselves with the product from the distillery of the Glaswegian who, in turn, had become increasingly touched by the generous gesture of his friend. When it was time to leave, the man from Glasgow felt moved to say something.

'I really appreciate it that you chose my whisky to drink instead of your own. It was a very kind thought.'

Please think nothing of it,' answered the Perth man. 'After all, it would not have been right to go to a funeral smelling of drink!'

The forerunner of the Excise man was the 'ale conner' who was appointed by local courts to visit all the alehouses and test each brew to make sure that it was 'good for men's bodies.' When he was given a pint of ale, tradition has it that he poured a little of it onto the alehouse bench before sitting on it. He then enjoyed the remainder of his drink, and perhaps a few more, at his leisure. Eventually, when it was time to rise, he knew that the brew was a worthy one if his leather breeches stuck to the bench. If no such adhesion was experienced, then the brew failed the test.

When a brew was approved, an 'ale garland', made up of flowers and greenery, was attached to the alehouse sign to advertise the good news to the drinking public. Ale conners date back to the time of William the Conqueror and I imagine that they must have been highly sought-after posts. In the 16th century, John Shakespeare was employed as an ale-taster in Stratford, before the birth of his more famous son William.

Another famous spiller of drinks was the 11th century Persian tent maker, Omar Khayyam. He was clearly fond of a drink but before raising his glass to his lips, he would always pour a little into the ground with the intention that it would soak through to quench the thirst of some poor drinking man, long deceased. Since death comes to all, he was very much in favour of enjoying life while he could. I can easily identify with his thoughts in the third verse of his illuminating, poetical work, the *Rubaiyat* –

'And, as the Cock crew, those who stood before
The Tavern shouted – 'Open then the Door!
You know how little while we have to stay,
And, once departed, may return no more!'

– which shows that some things have not changed very much over the last thousand years.

One of the best known, though perhaps least likely Excise man, from days gone by, was the Scottish poet, Robert Burns. The first tax on spirits was passed by the English Parliament in 1643 to help pay for the Civil War. A year later, the tax was extended to Scotland. This event immediately criminalised the activities of innumerable owners of small whisky stills all over the country. The authorities had discovered a 'wonderful' source of revenue which could be milked right up until the present day. However, collecting this duty was easier said than done. By the late 17th century, the effect of the tax had been to promote illicit stills and smuggling on a monumental scale. The response to this was the

Excise Officer – not the quaint figure in the leather breeches but well organised forces of heavily armed officers.

Robert Burns was appointed Officer of Excise in 1789 and in 1791, he became Officer, Dumfries 1st Foot Walk. In one engagement in 1792, he waded into the Solway, sword in hand, at the head of a group of officers, and boarded a smuggling brig. He placed the crew under arrest and conveyed the vessel to Dumfries, where it was sold. The official record reads – 'The Poet, does pretty well,' and in 1794, he was approved for promotion to Supervisor but sadly died two years later before the next vacancy occurred. But perhaps he still had the last laugh, with his famous poem – *The De'il's awa' wi' the Exciseman*, (or for the benefit of Sassenachs, such as myself – *The Devil is away with the Excise man*).

The De'il cam fiddling thro' the town,
And danced awa' wi' the Exciseman;
And ilka wife cried, 'Auld Mahoun,
We wish you luck o' your prize, man.'

We'll mak our maut, and brew our drink,
We'll dance, and sing, and rejoice, man;
And mony thanks to the muckle black De'il
That danced awa' wi' the Exciseman.

There's threesome reels, and foursome reels,
There's hornpipes and strathspeys, man;
But the ae best dance e'er cam to our lan',
Was – the De'il's awa' wi' the Exciseman.

One responsibility that I did not anticipate, was the very pleasant task of escorting visiting parties of the general public around the brewery. Some of these were day-time visits and others came in the evening. Whichever brewer was on duty would be roped in for this and I gladly took my turn.

The parties were usually met at the brewery gates and taken to a large illuminated flow chart in the foyer. Here, they were given a swift summary of the brewing process and then shown around the brewery, from the mill room to the bottling hall. After this was completed, the important business of the trip began. They were taken down to the Vaults. This was a visitor's hospitality bar located in the depth of the cellars. It was a place where, while ever people drank, beer was served and of course, it went without saying, the beer in the Vaults was *always* in perfect condition.

The décor of the Vaults included some interesting features. Running along the length of the walls were fitted oak benches and the bar itself, bulging out like the side of an enormous cask, had been specially made by one of the coopers. On the walls hung oil paintings of some of the last great Tennant's dray horses. These had been painted by an art student, many years earlier, who had been employed as a casual worker over the summer holidays. Someone must have had the good sense to realise that this worker would be better occupied with a brush and palate rather than a brush and shovel.

In the corner of the Vaults stood a small, round table which was described to visitors as the most expensive piece of furniture in the brewery. The reason for this was that the single pedestal that supported the table had been made from a piece of cylindrical core from a bore hole in the brewery yard. A few years earlier, an attempt had been made to drill for water. Unfortunately, nothing was found that was suitable for brewing and although the project had cost hundreds of thousands of pounds, all the brewery had to show for it was the table.

One of the first parties that I took round was a group of primary school children. (Safety regulations would probably not allow such a trip these days.) Their teacher was a very attractive young lady who, as was the fashion at that time, wore a very short skirt. It gave me a great deal of pleasure to watch her safely down the many spiral staircases that I made sure were on our route. Later, as we crossed the yard to the bottling department, one of the draymen on seeing the children, called across, 'Are they all yours, Frank?'

On this occasion, lemonade had been made available in the Vaults for the children and teacher, but usually only endless supplies of beer were provided. Most parties found this very acceptable but there was one time when it caused a bit of a problem. I had taken a party of ladies from the Women's Institute around the brewery and when we eventually settled into the Vaults, a group of ladies asked if they could have cups of tea. I apologised, explaining that we did not have the facilities for tea-making in the cellars and that most people who visited the brewery were keen to taste the 'product'. They declined the offer and while they sat quietly without a drink in front of them, another group of ladies were taking to the ale with great enthusiasm.

When the alcohol started to hit the mark, the drinking ladies started to make derogatory remarks about their non-drinking colleagues, on how miserable they were etc. The abstaining ladies, in their turn, looked askance at their inebriate friends, muttering about how they were showing themselves up. As the time wore on, I found my position, occupying the widening chasm between the two camps, increasingly uncomfortable and I was very relieved when it was time for them to go home.

One party who were unanimous in their appreciation of the hospitality given, were a group of young people from Norway. They partook of the ale with great relish and when it was almost time for them to leave, one of their number stood up and made an eloquent speech thanking me and the brewery for our hospitality. I spoke a few words in response, during the course of which I used the Norwegian word, *takk* for thanks. (I had recently been on holiday to that beautiful land.) They were surprisingly impressed by my linguistic skill. They said that no-one ever bothered to learn Norwegian. As a reward, they sang a long and beautiful song to me – none of which could I understand. I did not have the heart to tell them that *takk* was the one and only Norwegian word that I knew.

On another occasion, I was given the pleasure of escorting the comedian, Les Dawson, around the brewery. At that time, one of the trade union officials in the distribution department was also called Les Dawson. Someone must have had the idea that it would be good publicity if *our* Les Dawson met *the* Les Dawson, who happened to be appearing in one of the theatres in the town. After the local reporters and photographers had finished with him, Les accepted an invitation to have a look around the brewery and I was introduced to him.

I was pleasantly surprised to discover that his attitude was quite down-to-earth. He asked me if we employed many electricians because he had been a 'sparks' before doing what he was now engaged in. As we moved through the brewery, men greeted him and asked him about his 'mother-in-law' etc. He was quite happy to take the time to respond in a way appropriate to his stage persona. He didn't act like a star; he didn't need to: he was a star.

Frank with Les Dawson on his visit to the Tennant Brother's Brewery. "You don't have to be comedian to work in a brewery... but it helps!"

One party that I won't forget was a group of German students. They were very pleasant young people, but after we had been enjoying the hospitality of the Vaults for some time, one of them became conspicuous by his enthusiasm for his homeland.

'Did you know that in Germany, we make the best beer in the world?'

'I think it's all a matter of taste really,' I replied diplomatically, but I thought that his assertion was a touch discourteous, coming from one who had been partaking of our generosity so readily.

'Do you have any beer festivals in this country?'

'No,' I replied. 'If we want to have a drink, we just go to the nearest pub.'

'In Germany, we have many beer festivals.'

'That's nice,' I said, with forced enthusiasm.

'Do you have any special, commemorative beers?'

'No, not really,' I said.

'In Germany, we have many commemorative beers.'

By now he was really 'getting on my tits' (if you'll forgive the expression). Then I suddenly remembered something.

'Now I come to think of it, we do have a commemorative beer.' I directed him to a small display cabinet in the far corner of the Vaults. In pride of place was a rather dusty half pint bottle with an old-fashioned oval label, which proclaimed that it contained Tennants No 1 Strong. (Strong ales such as this were usually put into third of a pint, nip bottles.) In addition to the oval label, there was a second one wrapped around the shoulder of the bottle. This label displayed the Tennants coat of arms above the words, 'Tennant's Sheffield' and across the label, in distinct capital letters was the word 'VICTORY' and the dates 1939 and 1945. I can only assume that this satisfied my young Lederhosen'd friend's curiosity, since he did not ask any more questions during what remained of a very pleasant drinking session.

Some of the most interesting parties from a social point of view were those that took place in the evening, when all the senior staff were safely out of the way. This was particularly true when the parties were groups of young ladies, such as nurses or hairdressers. When you bring women and drink together, two things happen. Firstly, the women quickly lose their inhibitions and secondly, they find that they want to go for a pee – usually in pairs. The only toilet in the brewery suitable for women was a small 'single seater' in the corner of the yard. I found myself, then, frequently taking giggly girls up in the lift to the ground floor – a situation highly conducive to innocent amorousness. Even more opportunities arose outside the loo door when the second girl was waiting for the first to finish. I was sometimes taken by surprise by the frantic passion of their responses, but in retrospect, I now wonder if this had less to do with my undoubted charm and more to do with the fact that they were bursting for a pee.

Frank dipping the hopback at the Sheffield Brewery to check the volume of the brew.

Although these shenanigans were thankfully out of sight of higher management, they were not totally unobserved. Many windows looked down upon the brewery yard. As Jeff, one of the fermenting room shift men commented later one evening, 'If H.B. ever saw what you've been up to, he'd have your guts for garters.' But I had the confidence of one who had enjoyed a good few drinks. As Burns said, 'Twill make your courage rise.'

The Head Brewer, Harold Burkinshaw, had himself taken parties around the brewery in his younger days. In a relaxed moment, he once told me about an incident with a lady in one of his groups. The tour of the brewery had been completed and they were having a drink in the cellar when a rather 'well built' lady asked if she could go to the toilet. (You are not allowed to call people 'fat' these days – those who are politically correct, bless them, would probably have called this lady, 'circumferencely challenged'.)

The incident occurred in the days before the lift had been installed in the brewery and H.B. decided to take her by the most direct route to the ground floor which was up one of the many iron, spiral staircases. This particular one was rather narrow and after the lady had mounted a few of the steps, she became firmly stuck, her 'width' being securely held by the hand rails. She could neither advance nor retreat. H.B., resourceful as ever, summoned two wiry cellar men to the scene. They stepped up behind the lady and each of them shouldered one of her generous buttocks. One stair at a time, they eased her up, like pushing a cork out of a bottle, until she was free, at the top. Another satisfied customer!

In addition to working a three shift system, it was also my responsibility to provide weekend cover at the brewery every two or three weeks. This involved being present from 8am to noon on Saturday and Sunday mornings to check the fermentations and to supervise the extensive cleaning that took place during these hours. It was also necessary to call in at 8pm on these days to check the fermentations again. Such frequent visits clearly restricted one's social life on duty weekends. However, I managed to find a way of combining business with pleasure.

I lived about six miles from the brewery and whichever route I took there were a large number of public houses between the brewery gate and my home. So on Saturday evenings, after finishing at the brewery, I would walk home, calling in to as many pubs as I could manage before closing time.

Some of the pubs were our own, but many of them were those of our competitors – Stone's, Ward's and Tetley's. At that time, our main competition came from Stone's Bitter. It was known locally as 'Jungle Juice' because it tended to give you a headache. In those days, it was considered that you hadn't had a decent drink of an evening if you didn't wake up with a decent hangover the next morning.

Whatever the case, my routine was the same. I would order a half of the best bitter and while it was being dispensed, I'd look behind the bar to see what bottled beers and other drinks were offered for sale. I'd notice how many people were in the pub, what sort of people they were, what they were drinking and whether they seemed to be enjoying themselves. I'd watch whether they were drinking quickly or if they were the sort of customers who sit behind the same half emptied glass all night. I'd look at the décor to see if it was traditional or modern, whether it was clean and comfortable or cheap and tatty. I would observe the bar staff to see if they were clean and capable of serving a glass of beer satisfactorily and that they were friendly without being over-familiar – I hate being referred to as 'Squire' by pub staff. Finally, and most importantly, I'd pick up my drink and judge whether the glass was clean and contained the correct volume and then I would drink it in the hope that it satisfied all the rigorous standards that I had come to expect in a good glass of ale.

This routine quickly became second nature to me, so much so, that almost forty years on, I still find myself carrying it out whenever I visit a public house which, thankfully, is quite often.

As the evening drew on and the number of visits increased, this 'quality control' routine progressively became less defined –

perhaps even fuzzy. The pubs were getting more crowded and in some of them there was entertainment. The days of upright pianos and 'acoustic' singing had all but disappeared in city pubs. Now it was electronic keyboards and singers with hand held microphones. I remember one such performance in which an early Tom Jones song was being murdered by a singer and a keyboard player who seemed to be trying to drown each other out. Their respective pieces of equipment must have been turned on to full volume. The ear splitting rendition was enough to shake the flaky paintwork off the ceiling. The song ended to rapturous relief and silence. The part-time Master of Ceremonies took the microphone.

'The singing was wonderful but the applause was terrible,' he chuckled nervously. He began to introduce the next song. I squinted across at the dartboard on the opposite wall.

'Is that the time already?' I mumbled. 'I think it's time I moved on.' As I walked homewards, I could sometimes catch a glimpse, between the houses, of the crescent moon laid back like a drunken banana.

6

Qualifications and Experience

My duties as a Production Supervisor were virtually the same as those of the brewers. The only difference was that I had no formal brewing qualifications – but I was working on it.

To go back a few years, after I had left school in 1959, I was aware of the fact that I had only narrowly missed passing the 'A' level examinations in Biology and Chemistry and since I surmised that these might be useful qualifications for my chosen career, I had signed on at night school to study them again with a view to re-sitting the examinations.

In 1960, a few months after I had joined the brewery, the Head Brewer had arranged for me to attend a series of six evening lectures on 'Brewing Microbiology' at Burton-on-Trent Technical College. The papers were presented by scientists pre-eminent in their field, including our own Eric Wiles whose lecture was entitled, 'Wild Yeast Encountered in Breweries'.

The choice of Burton-on-Trent as a venue was highly appropriate since the town was dominated by brewing. There was the giant Bass Brewery, displaying its red triangle on the brewery tower, Ind Coope's brewery, brewing Double Diamond – a popular national beer at the time and the more modest but none the less very traditional brewery of Marston, Thomson & Evershed, now known as Marston's. There may well have been others, but I did not see them.

Burton had been famous for brewing since the monks of Burton Abbey – founded in 1002 by Wulfric Spot, Earl of Mercia – discovered that its 'gypseous' well waters were eminently suited to the brewing of excellent ales. Alfred Barnard visited thirteen breweries and several maltings in the town around 1889. Of the town, he wrote:

'No one can form an accurate idea of the Beer Town who has not paid it a visit. Almost every large structure is either a brewhouse or some building connected, directly or indirectly, with the manufacture of beer. The very streets are made subservient to the business, for, not only are they crossed and recrossed by railway lines, but if a house or shop should happen to stand in the way of a brewery extension, it is doomed and very quickly demolished... Seventy per cent of the entire population are employed in the breweries, and upon the whole they are thrifty and well to do, not withstanding their occupation and the temptation to drink.'

In addition to its superlative natural waters, Burton-on-Trent had another claim to fame: the Burton Union system. This was a fermentation method that had probably developed from the old farmhouse brewing system in which the same vessel often had to carry out several different functions such as mashing and fermentation etc. In the Burton Union system, beer was fermented in large wooden casks. As the fermentation proceeded, the excess yeast and froth that was produced was discharged from the top bungholes, via 'swan neck' pipes into a trough which was situated above the casks. Beer, separating from this yeast, drained back into the cask via another pipe fitted into the lower hole.

Compared to open squares or even the Dropping System, the Burton Union System was quite labour intensive, as it needed a great deal of care and attention to make sure that all parts of the plant were kept clean and free from infection. However, it produced a beer of particularly fine flavour and the yeast crop obtained was highly

The Burton Union System. A labour intensive method in which beer is fermented in large wooden casks.

vigorous. In a subsequent visit to a Burton brewery, I was shown a room containing a hundred or more operating Burton Union sets, arranged in rows. Over the years, the use of the system has declined. In 1982, the Bass brewery discontinued its use and I believe that the only brewery where the system may be found today is Marston's, who use it in the brewing of Owd Rodger and Pedigree.

In 1961, I had passed 'A' level Biology and in 1962, I had passed the Chemistry examination at the same level. Around the same time, the Head Brewer had arranged another outing for me, this time a two-week visit to the Brewing Industry Research Foundation at Lyttel Hall, Nutfield in Surrey. The Foundation had been established in 1951 and was fostered and financed by the brewing industry. It carried research on 'the raw materials of brewing and the nature of the processes leading to their transformation into beer'.

Once at Lyttel Hall, I was well looked after by a young man called Lesley Hawkins who showed me around all the departments, explained what was happening in each or them and introduced me to other scientific staff. Coming from an old traditional brewery, I was fascinated by the research that was being carried out at the cutting edge of brewing technology. A large number of technical papers were produced and many of these were stored in a room above the library – where Lesley and I were sitting one afternoon. We happened to overhear a conversation between two staff members concerning the room above.

'It must be quite a weight now,' said the first, looking nervously at the ceiling. 'There must be a limit to the amount we can store up there.' 'Yes there is,' replied the second. 'It's when the ceiling falls down.'

It was refreshing to be in the presence of the academic mind.

The fashionable topic for research in those days was 'Continuous Brewing', as opposed to the batch brewing that had been carried out for centuries, if not millennia. People were investigating such devices as continuous mashing machines and continuous hop extractors. Lesley Hawkins was working on a continuous fermenting vessel.

The fermentation, which took place in a completely enclosed tank, was kept active by a series of rotating paddles. Fresh wort was slowly introduced into the vessel via a pipe at one end and fermented beer issued forth from a pipe at the other end. By varying the rate of flow, beers of different character could be obtained from sweet, partly fermented to fully fermented, dry flavours. The problem with continuous fermentation was sterility. If just one beer-spoilage micro-organism managed to get into the system, it would have time to multiply to unacceptable levels. However, during the time I was there, the system was producing some very drinkable beer.

Because the beer was produced purely for experimental purposes rather than for sale, it was not necessary to pay any duty on it and although some of it was diverted to other departments, much of it was available for consumption, and very nice it was too. Since the experiment was restricted to investigating the fermentation system, no hops had been used. I fancied I was drinking something akin to Old English ale, brewed at a time before hops were cultivated in this country and changed the name of our national drink to beer and changed its flavour forever.

Brewing folklore has it that when Flemish weavers came over to England in the 16th century to escape religious persecution, they brought with them a taste for hop flavoured ale which they called beer. This was the start of hop cultivation and 'beer' brewing in Britain. However, in truth, it was not quite as simple as that. Hopped beer had been brewed in England prior to the arrival of the Flemings and as far back as Saxon times, hops, which were known to grow wild in the hedgerows, were believed to have been sometimes used in the brewing of ale. The Flemish immigrants certainly introduced the commercial cultivation of hops in Kent around 1524 and so started an industry that would thrive for more than four centuries. But support for hopped beer was by no means universal at first. Around 1530, a song with the catchy title of, *High and Mightie Commendation of the Virtue of a Pot of Good Ale,* was written. I quote the first verse below:

> *And in very deed, the hops but a weed*
> *Brought over 'gainst law, and here set to sale,*
> *Would the law were removed, and no more Beer brewed,*
> *But all good men betake them to a pot of good ale.*

However, drinkers soon learned to appreciate that a flavour that balanced the mellow sweetness of malt with the delicate bitterness of English grown hops was the finest flavour in the world. In addition to this, brewers discovered that when hops were used in brewing, the product remained in good condition for longer. Hops acted as a preservative. A sixteenth century hop enthusiast wrote: 'For if your Ale may endure a fortnight, your Beere through the benefit of the hop shall continue a month, and what grace it yieldeth to the taste all men may judge that have sense in them.'

Today the term beer generally refers to any alcoholic drink made by fermenting malted barley and sometimes other cereals. Ale on the other hand, is usually confined to British and Irish beers and does not include stout, porter or lager.

During the time that I was working in the bottling laboratory I had been given the chance to visit *Brew-X*, the brewing exhibition that was regularly held in one of the large exhibition venues in London. Most of the production staff would be going, although in order to minimise disruption to the running of the brewery, people from the same departments would, as far as was possible, go on different days of the week. In other words, our visits would be 'staggered'.

Brew-X was an opportunity for the many companies that supplied the brewing industry with raw materials, plant or services, to show what new innovations they could offer. It was their chance to strengthen links with existing customers and to forge new links with potential ones, all in a very convivial atmosphere. Since I was going to be travelling down alone, colleagues advised me that there would be a lot of drink about and that it should be quite an enjoyable session.

I was not disappointed. Not only were there several bars in the exhibition hall, but many of the exhibitors were offering 'hospitality' on their stands. I got around as many stands as I could and I accepted as much hospitality as I could manage and by the time I made my way back to the station for the return journey I was pleasantly relaxed. I was not drunk. Brewery people do not get drunk; they get 'relaxed', (just as politicians get 'tired and emotional'). I am reminded of the poem, *Not Drunk is He*. I don't know where it comes from – I seem to have known it all my life.

Not drunk is he who from the floor
Can rise again and drink some more
But drunk is he who prostrate lies
And can neither drink nor rise.

The train back to Sheffield was not due for half an hour or so and as I sat on a bench waiting, the thought came to me that this had been my first visit to *Brew-X* and if I were asked what I thought about it, I estimated that by tomorrow, I would not remember a single thing. So, in order to remedy this, I leafed through my crumpled copy of the exhibition guide and tried to remember which stands I had visited. I identified about five or six and then I wrote a few notes in the margins, describing what they had to offer.

About a week later, the Head Brewer sent a memorandum to all those who had been to the exhibition, requesting a report from each of us. He wanted to know what new developments had been on display and how these could be of benefit to our own brewery. He outlined five or six headings on which to base our reports. I frantically dug out my exhibition guide which was by now, very crumpled and found I was able to draft out a passable report. Those, almost illegible, spidery notes had succeeded in saving my bacon.

So, the foregoing reminiscences represent the qualifications and experience I had gained up to the time of becoming a Production Supervisor. Now that I was working alongside the brewers, Harold Burkinshaw, the Head Brewer, suggested that I should work towards acquiring some brewing qualifications. The Institute of Brewing, which had been founded in 1886 as 'The Laboratory Club', was the professional body responsible for maintaining academic standards in the industry. They set and administered brewing examinations.

Since membership of the Institute was open to all technical staff involved in brewing and malting, I was already an ordinary member, of several years standing. They advised me that I would first need to sit the Associate Membership Qualifying Examination, which consisted of three papers – Biochemistry, Microbiology and Physics, but since I already held an 'A' level in Physics I was exempt from the last of these. Consequently, I launched myself into a programme of self-study to cover the syllabuses of the first two.

My next trip out was a two week visit to Sandar's Maltings. Looking back, I can see now that my career was developing in a logical direction. As I persevered with my academic education, Harold Burkinshaw was providing the opportunities, by means of informative outside visits, for me to gain the appropriate experience to compliment my studies. I was not aware of it at the time; it just seemed to happen by chance, but I appreciate it now.

Sandar's had two maltings, one in Gainsborough and the other in Grimsby. The first week was spent at the Gainsborough plant which operated some of the most up-to-date and technically advanced malting equipment of the time. The notes and diagrams that I made, served me well a few years later when I was studying for the brewing diploma. My memories of Grimsby, where I spent the second week, were somewhat bitter-sweet. I was overjoyed to discover that it was a traditional floor malting, as these fast disappearing plants were becoming a rarity. On the other hand, the day I arrived there saw redundancy notices being given out to the men. Within a few weeks, it would be closed down.

Traditional malting took place in three stages – steeping, flooring and kilning. First the barley was soaked in water in tanks or 'steeps' until it had absorbed between 40 to 50 per cent moisture. The old maltsters could assess this by squeezing it between his thumb and forefinger. When this had been achieved, the water was drained away and the grain was spread on the malting floor to the depth of two or three feet. Malting floors, which were of extensive area, were arranged one above the other, in purpose-built buildings, to form a series of low ceilinged rooms with shuttered windows around the walls for ventilation. There were often rows of pillars running along the rooms for reinforcement. Once the grain was on the floor, it would begin to germinate – fine rootlets would start to grow from one end of the corn and later, a shoot would emerge from the other. The process of converting starch to fermentable malt sugar that was beginning now, would be completed in the brewery mash tun.

Germination caused the temperature to rise and it was important to prevent the batch or 'piece' from over-heating. This was achieved by 'turning the piece'. Men with broad wooden shovels or 'skips' edged systematically along the floor, rhythmically tossing the grain into the air. If the grain needed to be cooled, they spread the piece out to make it shallower. Conversely, if it was too cool, they deepened the piece so that it warmed up. Not only did this skilful procedure maintain the correct temperature but it prevented the piece from becoming matted together by the growing rootlets.

At Grimsby, I was invited to have a go at 'turning the piece'. I very quickly learned that not only was it a difficult procedure to

A depiction of traditional floor malting, where the men are rhythmically tossing the grain to the air so as to maintain the correct temperature.

master but it was also very tiring. Although I was young and fit in those days, in a short time I was in need of a rest. Among the malting men, there was an old lad who wore an ancient striped blazer which, in better days, would not have looked out of place on the pages of Jerome K. Jerome's *Three Men in a Boat*. This elderly man made the task look easy. The shovel seemed to be an extension of his arms which swung effortlessly to the sway of his body. The other men said that he could keep on like that all day long and I had no reason to disbelieve them. It was yet another traditional skill which is now all-but lost forever.

When the flooring process was complete, at which stage the newly grown shoot would have extended two thirds the length of the corn, the 'green malt' as it was called, was ready for kilning. It was dried in this way to arrest any further growth and to render it into a suitable condition to be delivered to a brewery. Kiln roofs were characteristically pyramidal or pagoda shaped, with a ventilator at the top. Such structures, adjoining traditional breweries and distilleries today, proclaim their intended use.

Included in the workforce of the Grimsby maltings was a cat. I say the 'workforce' because the animal was not employed as a pet – it was expected to work for its living. In such an old building with so much grain around, it was inevitable that rodents would be attracted to it. A resident cat was an easy, cheap and safe solution to the problem. Not only maltings but often traditional breweries and distilleries had cats to keep them free from rats and mice. Some of these felines became part of legend.

Robinson's Brewery of Stockport named its beer 'Old Tom' (which was first brewed in 1899) after the brewery cat and at the Old Jameson Distillery in Dublin, their cat was stuffed (taxidermically) in recognition of the fact that it had rid the premises of well over a thousand mice. I am assured that the honour was delayed until the old cat had finally passed on to that 'big distillery in the sky'. There was not a cat at the Sheffield brewery during my time there but there was an old story going the rounds, on the subject.

One night as the old tom-cat was patrolling the brewery, he was walking along the edge of a vat full of beer when he noticed something splashing about. It was a little mouse.

'Please save me!' cried the mouse, 'I'm drowning.'

'Don't be silly,' answered the cat. 'If I saved you, I would feel compelled to eat you.'

'I don't mind that so much,' replied the little mouse. 'It's a natural way to go, but drowning is the very last thing I want to do.'

'Very well,' said the cat, 'but only if you agree to let me eat you.'

'Agreed!' shrieked the mouse.

The old cat extended his tail across the surface of the beer to the little mouse who grabbed it, climbed up onto the cat's back and then onto his head. He quickly jumped onto a pipe and ran along it and dived into his hole in the wall.

'I say!' exclaimed the indignant cat. 'You've broken your promise.'

The mouse peeped out and replied, 'Yes I know. I'm really sorry but the truth is, you just can't believe a word I say, when I've got some beer inside me.'

At Highland Park distillery on Orkney, they have been 'employing' cats for 200 years to keep the mice down. In March 2006, a ginger tom called Barley, the last in a long line of cats, sadly passed away. Due to new health and safety rules, Barley was not replaced. Let us hope that brewery/distillery/maltings cats do not go the way of the cooper and yet another traditional skill is lost forever.

In June 1968, I was notified that I had passed the Associate Membership Qualifying Examination and the following January, I was elected an Associate Member of the Institute of Brewing. Besides the Institute, there was another professional body serving the industry. It was the Incorporated Brewers' Guild, which had been founded in 1906 by a group of Yorkshire brewers and included a benevolent society 'for the relief of distress amongst its members'. Unlike the Institute, membership of the Guild was confined solely to working brewers. Consequently, I was pleased to be elected a student member of the Guild in June, 1968 and then be transferred to ordinary membership in March, 1969.

The next stage in my education was to start studying for the Institute's highest qualification, the Diploma. It was far more comprehensive than the Associate examination. It would be necessary to sit six papers on subjects such as Malting, Brewing, Processing, Packaging, Quality Control and Engineering. It was going to be hard work.

At that time, Whitbread & Co. still had a policy of training young graduates to become brewers and since the Sheffield brewery combined much that was traditional with a sprinkling of modern innovations, many, if not all of these young men were sent to us to carry out their year's pupilage. Invariably, they found themselves placed 'under my wing' since I was the youngest member of the production team and due to my 'constant' studying, I had a useful selection of technical facts at my fingertips.

One of these pupils was Roddy Llewelyn, son of the Olympic equestrian, Captain Harry Llewelyn who was at that time Managing Director of Whitbread International. (We also had our very own Olympic champion; table-tennis playing Derek Riches, who was the Brewer's Clerk at Sheffield, reached the quarter-finals in Tokyo and won the bronze medal at the Toronto Olympics.) I gained the impression that Roddy did not share his father's enthusiasm for a career in the brewing industry. Nevertheless, he persevered with patience and uncommon courtesy.

During the year that Roddy was with us, I enjoyed many social outings with him but I discovered that he did have one flaw. Although he could speak several languages fluently, his extensive education had not prepared him for the subtleties of the Sheffield dialect. I found him one lunchtime 'stumped' by the request, 'Aztha gorra tanner?' coming from a workman at the canteen ticket machine. I explained to him that the man was asking him if he would lend him a 'six penny piece'.

Some time later, the brewery was humming with some rather unsettling news. Whitbread's was going to discontinue brewing at Bentley's Yorkshire Brewery in Woodlesford. It was argued that since it was a small brewery and that nearby Kirkstall Brewery had spare brewing capacity, it made sense to rationalise production in this way. Two large modern fermenting vessels had recently been installed at Kirkstall. We subsequently learned that Fred Knight, the brewer responsible for the day to day running of the Woodlesford brewery had been found a post somewhere else in the group and consequently, they were going to be a brewer short, up until the time that brewing ceased. As a result, I found myself suddenly being dispatched up to Woodlesford to 'hold the fort' until other arrangements could be made.

The brewery had been founded in 1828 by Henry Bentley on seven and a half acres of land. The location had been selected because of the presence of the Eshald Well that was located on the site and was known to be a reliable source of excellent water. The brewery became known as Eshald Well Brewery. In the 19th century, it consisted of an extensive brewhouse, spacious cellars, numerous workshops, cooperages and stables and six maltings. It was not only served by road and canal, on which the brewery had its own barges, but it also had its own branch line of the Midland Railway.

Henry Bentley was the son of the famous Huddersfield brewer, Timothy Bentley who had built the first maltings at Woodlesford in 1808. It was he who had invented the Yorkshire Square. This was a square fermenting vessel divided into two chambers by a horizontal deck about three quarters of the way up the vessel. The larger, lower chamber was filled with pitched wort and the yeast head escaped through a porthole into the upper chamber. Wort in the yeast head drained back into the lower chamber through an outlet known as the 'organ pipe'. A certain amount of rousing was often necessary, but when the fermentation was complete the porthole was closed and the beer was racked off, leaving the yeast behind in the upper chamber. Beers fermented in this way, drank very full for their gravity – in other words, they seemed stronger than they really were.

Yorkshire Squares are still used in some Yorkshire breweries, including Sam Smith's Brewery at Tadcaster, Yorkshire's oldest brewery – having been established in 1758. I understand that they are also being used at the Black Sheep Brewery in Masham and in Tetley's Brewery in Leeds, where some 'modern' Yorkshire Squares have been installed.

When I arrived at the Woodlesford brewery, I found that I was left very much to my own devices. This was a refreshing change and when I came across an old microscope in the brewing office, I used it to examine the samples of the yeast crop. I then used

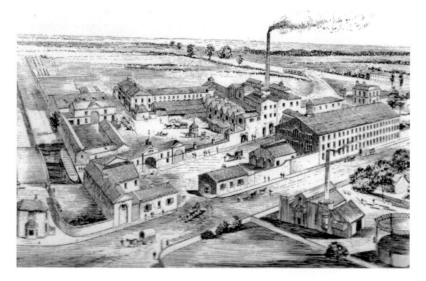

Bentley's Yorkshire Brewery in Woodlesford.

these results to select the best yeast for saving for subsequent brews. However, I nearly came undone when I mashed on the first brew. I had turned on the liquor and opened the grist slide and the mash was pouring into the mash-tun at the correct consistency. It was now only necessary to fine tune the temperature which, as I have explained earlier, is crucial to the quality of the beer.

When I scrutinised the mashing thermometer, I was dumbfounded to discover that there were no numbers on it. Against each graduation was a letter of the alphabet! The old brewers had had these unique thermometers made in order to protect the secrets of their brewing from competitors. I discovered later that the special code needed to decipher the temperature was 'God B My Help'. Fortunately, the brewery foreman, Albert Clegg, was at hand to put me right and together we finished the mash satisfactorily. A week or so later, we were able to taste the brew in the sample room and assure ourselves that the high standards set by Henry Bentley had been maintained.

Yorkshiremen have always been proud of their beer and have enjoyed drinking it. It is said that in 1761, Henry Elwes, a Yorkshireman, died after drinking two thousand gallons of ale from a brown jug. That sounds like quite a good session, even for a Yorkshireman. After his death, he became known as Toby Fillpot and this became the nickname for any drinker of distinction. His image was used in the development of the Toby Jug in which he was portrayed as a 'well made' man wearing a long, open coat and a three cornered hat and grasping a jug of ale. This depiction of the enjoyment of English ale must be one of the most enduring features in English pottery and indeed Hoare's Red Lion Brewery of Lower East Smithfield, London, used it as a symbol for many years before they registered it as a trade mark in 1907. In 1933, Charrington's Brewery of London merged with Hoare's and continued to use it both as a trade mark and as the name of one of their beers.

In 1972, Whitbread's launched a company newspaper in the region, called the *East Pennines Post*. They were keen to attract as many contributions as possible and, as a result, I felt prompted to write a series of short stories under the title of *Tales of Ferment*. The first one, which appeared in issue number one, is reproduced below:

Though familiarity may breed contempt between men and women, this fortunately is not the case between men and beer. The 'never again' of the morning after is never fulfilled and by the evening, the infatuation for that frothy-headed charmer down at the local is back in full flood. Similarly, a man working all day in the brewery with sticky, smelly, foaming, bubbling beer will, after his work is done, rush eagerly to the idyllic surroundings of the nearest ale house and purchase that sparkling nectar which is our bread and butter.

A few weeks ago, one such man left the brewery after the Saturday morning shift and entered the portals of the Lady's Bridge Hotel in Sheffield, a charming tavern on the bank of the noble Don.

'A pint of Trophy, luv,' he called to the barman, who served him immediately. He downed the pint in three seconds flat, slapped the empty glass on the counter and called, 'Same agee'en!' He was served with another pint which he dispatched with equal haste.

'Ast tha ollus drunk like that?' enquired the curious barman.

'Only since me accidunt,' answered our hero.

'Oh, am sorry t'ear that. A dint mean ter pry,' apologised the barman, 'but wot did tha do?'

The man looked around quickly before answering, to see that no-one was listening. 'It were last Wednesday,' he said. 'A nokter fullen over!'

This was the first piece of writing that I ever got published and was the beginning of a hobby that would preserve my sanity in the turbulent years to come. A few months later, the *East Pennines Post* asked for readers views on the paper and this resulted in my first-ever favourable review in print. Around this time, I began writing a novel, *The Bubble*, which described the fate of a traditional, northern brewery which was threatened with takeover by a national, London-based group. Although it took me many years to complete, the plot was rather predictable and in retrospect, I am not surprised that I was unable to get it published.

However, my main preoccupation at the time was to study for the Diploma. Working in a brewery that was largely traditional, I was aware of the fact that my knowledge of the latest technical innovations was somewhat limited. So when I found that I had a day's leave due, I arranged to visit Kirkstall Brewery to examine the workings of their modern fermenting vessels. Although the main part of the brewery was quite old (signatures carved in the old stone walls dated back to 1832), Whitbread's had installed some conical-bottomed fermenting vessels to increase their brewing capacity.

These large, enclosed vessels were very much favoured by the company. They had installed them at the giant brewery at Luton. which had been opened in 1969 and was the first entirely new brewery to be built in Britain for well over thirty years.

They were now installing them at the new brewery that was being built at Salmesbury, near Preston. Here, each vessel had a capacity of two thousand barrels. The 'conicals' at Kirkstall were of more modest dimensions but they were of the same basic design. They were tall, narrow, upright, cylindrical tanks, the bottoms of which were conical. They had a cooling jacket around them so that when the fermentation was complete, the beer could be cooled down and the suspended yeast would settle down into the cone. This yeast was then run off first before the beer was diverted to the next stage.

Although these vessels were tall, they only occupied a relatively small area of floor space and they had the additional advantage that should the brewery close down, they could be lifted out and transported to another brewery. Here, they could be set up in a suitable location in the open air and when installed, a prefabricated building constructed around them.

As I left Kirkstall, I noticed that the public house next to the brewery was called *The Bridge*. The two pubs nearest to Tennant's

Brewery were *The Bridge* and *The Lady's Bridge*. I recalled other breweries that had similarly named pubs in their vicinity. The truth of the matter was that many breweries were built next to rivers, so much so, that some cynics suggested that the brewers used the murky waters of town rivers to brew their beer with. Nothing could have been further from the truth. The embarrassing reality of the situation was that brewers often built their establishments next to rivers in order to have somewhere to flush away all their effluent.

In the Sheffield brewery, ten barrels of liquor were used to brew a single barrel of beer. Most of the excess was utilised in the rigorous cleaning programmes employed throughout the brewery and much of it finished up in the River Don which flowed alongside the premises. From time to time and completely unannounced, a man from the water board would appear on the scene, intent on checking the consistency of our effluent.

At the first sighting of the 'Drain Man', as he was called, whoever was on duty in the brewery would be dispatched around the plant to turn on as many hose pipes as possible and if their was any ecologically 'unfriendly' material around, such as yeast slurry, to hold it back until after the Drain Man had taken his samples and gone away. I feel sure that brewers today demonstrate a much more enlightened attitude towards the environment.

It was not only liquid effluent that was released into the river. On one occasion, the police were called in when a pedestrian on the bridge was convinced that he saw a severed hand caught on the weir. It turned out to be one of the coarse, red, industrial gloves that the men wore when they were handling corrosive cleaning materials. On another occasion, a sighting of a 'dead body' turned out to be a pair of trousers caught on an underwater obstacle and inflated by the current of the river. The old glove had doubtless been discarded by someone in the brewery, but the origins of the pair of trousers forever remained a mystery.

It would be wrong to think that all my trips out from the brewery were for the purposes of serious education. There were many social gatherings and expeditions; after all, the brewery was a close-knit community in which our colleagues were also our friends.

One evening a month, the production staff from the brewery and bottling department (those who were not on duty) plus the odd Excise Officer, were transported in a brewery van to a pub in Hoylandswaine, near Barnsley called, if I remember rightly, *The Lord Nelson*. A separate room was always reserved for our party and as soon as we arrived, large jugs of ale and glasses were brought in to us. There would be a constant stream of large jugs of ale throughout the evening. At one end of the room, there was always a generous table weighed down with tasty and tempting food which we availed ourselves of with great enthusiasm.

The last barrel of traditional draught is racked at Sheffield, 1974.

After this was finished and washed down with some more ale, a tournament was organised and played involving darts and dominoes (fives and threes). I seem to recall that this was often won by the most unlikely people.

When this was settled, there was a brief rest period when most of us sat down and caught up with our drinking to the accompaniment of *Fats Waller* tunes played delicately on an old piano by Ronnie Lumb. After this, some were inspired to recite ballads of the 'Eskimo Nell' variety and finally, when we were all pleasantly 'relaxed', we were brought together in community singing.

There was some attempt at sweet harmonies but we mostly gravitated towards bawdy ditties such as, *Cats on the Rooftops*.

> *Cats on the rooftops, cats on the tiles,*
> *Cats with syphilis, cats with piles,*
> *Cats with their arseholes - - , wreathed in smiles,*
> *As they revel in the joys of fornication.*
> *etc, etc.*

(This was sung very approximately to the tune of *D'ye Ken John Peel*)

Only a flimsy curtain separated our private room from the public bar area. I wonder if the customers realised that what they were hearing emanated from the cream of the local brewing industry.

Although angling was a very popular pastime in Sheffield, I had never been drawn to it. However, I had heard some very good reports about the brewery sea-angling trips to Bridlington and, against my better judgment, I was persuaded to join one. We met in the brewery yard quite early in the morning where the hired bus was waiting for us. I noticed that several cases of Gold Label shorts were being secreted under the passenger seats. As we left the sleeping city behind us, I felt that it was rather early in the day to be imbibing alcoholic beverages. Nevertheless, after a couple of mouthfuls, the barley wine started to go down rather readily.

Some time later however, we were all feeling quite uncomfortable in the bladder department. After some protracted persuasion, the driver agreed to look out for somewhere suitable to stop. He eventually pulled into a lay-by with the comment that we would have to go down the bank.

The first group out of the bus, seeing that the bank was steep and sludgy, decided upon a different course of action and began to relieve themselves against the side of the bus. The rest of us, who were by now outside, followed suit – after all, we did have our decent clothes on. When the driver noticed what was happening to his paintwork, he drew the bus forwards a few yards, revealing a line of men who were displaying to the world a degree of nonchalance, inappropriate to their predicament.

When we finally reached the town of Bridlington, we made our way to the harbour. The sight of 'our boat', when it was pointed out to me, caused me not a little concern. It was much smaller than I had expected. To my inexperienced eye, it looked little more than an elongated rowing boat with a small engine slung over the back end. Those who had been on these trips before, assured me that they usually went out on boats like this and so we all stumbled aboard.

Once we had left the glass-like waters of the harbour behind us, we found that the open sea was quite choppy. Each time that the front of the boat hit a wave, a great shower of drenching spray hit us. It was at this stage that one of our group pulled a meat pie from his bag and started to munch it. I wondered to myself whether this was a wise course of action in view of the movement of the sea, rising up around us.

The harbour and the town gradually receded into the distance and we finally stopped not far from Flamborough Head. Any hopes that this might signal a calming of the boat's movement, were cruelly dashed. We seemed to be located in a part of the sea that was characterised by a strong and uncomfortable swell and our pie-munching colleague was still munching; he seemed to have an inexhaustible supply of pies. The boat-man swayed across to each of us in that rocking craft to show us how to put the bait on our hooks and generally how to use the tackle provided. The serious business of fishing began.

We all laughed when the first man started to be sick over the side, but we did not laugh for long. One by one, most of us succumbed to that horrible experience. I (and many others) totally lost interest in the fishing. We would have paid a fortune to be back on dry land, but it was a condition of the trip that we had to stay out for the full-allotted time otherwise some people might claim a rebate. One cheerful soul pointed out that we could have booked it for longer, but the only replies he received were muttered obscenities from those who did not have their heads over the side of the boat at that particular moment. In one brief settled moment, I enquired why it was that we had come to this precise patch of sea, which was so turbulent. I was told that it was here where the fish would be found. They probably came here, I thought, to enjoy our long-lost breakfasts.

The interminable wait was pure torture but eventually, it was time to go back. Once we were moving again and pointing towards the harbour, spirits began to rise a little. Very few fish had been caught and the only man not to have been sick was the pie muncher. As we entered the harbour, we were almost cheerful and when we stepped onto the quayside, two things happened; firstly, our stomachs suddenly felt settled and secondly, our legs which had grown accustomed to the rolling of the sea, could not cope with solid ground and we staggered about like drunken men, so much so, that we had to find the nearest pub and drink enough beer to compensate for this effect. It should not be too surprising to learn that this was my one and only venture into the 'pleasures' of sea fishing.

In 1973, I learned that I had passed the Diploma examination. This was the highest qualification in the profession and I was subsequently elected Diploma Member of the Institute of Brewing and my membership of the Incorporated Brewers' Guild was elevated from Ordinary to Senior level. As a result, the company had no choice but to re-designate my status to that of a Brewer.

Brewing is sometimes described as the world's second oldest profession. This prompts one to make comparisons with the first oldest profession. Some say that women drive men to drink and indeed W.C.Fields once said, 'It was a woman that drove me to drink, but I never got the chance to thank her for it.' Personally, I think that it happens the other way around; that drink draws men to women. As the old saying has it:

'Drink makes men into poets and all women beautiful.'

7

First Taste of the North-East

One day, not long after I had gained my precious Diploma, the Head Brewer asked me to escort a rather special party around the brewery. It consisted of a group of shop stewards who had travelled down from the north-eastern reaches of Whitbread East Pennines, the brewery at Castle Eden. They had the reputation of being quite militant and were likely to take industrial action at the drop of a hat and so I approached the encounter with a mixture of caution and curiosity.

The purpose of their visit was to see for themselves the working conditions, such as working practices and wages, of their equivalent workers in Sheffield with a view to gaining parity with them. It was certainly true that the further one travelled from London, three things happened – the wages became progressively lower and the beer became stronger and cheaper. Unfortunately, the last two factors did not necessarily compensate for the first and our friends from the north-east were keen to remedy the wages imbalance – at least within the context of the East Pennines region.

I was to show them around the brewery and then take them down to the Vaults for a drink, but since H.B. would not be available to talk to them until late afternoon, I was instructed to take my time and give them the full tour so that they did not spend too much time drinking. He did not wish to be confronted by drunken shop stewards. Once the men were settled in the Vaults, it was suggested that I should introduce them to our own brewery shop steward, Jock McKinnon, so that they could have a chat with him until H.B. could get down to them.

The first thing I noticed when I met the group was how many there were of them – half a dozen or so – representing a brewery not much more than a third of the size of the Sheffield brewery. The second surprise was how good humoured and reasonable they were, not at all like the ogres I had been led to expect. We chatted quite amiably and it was agreed that I would describe each part of the brewery as though they were strangers to the industry, even though this meant that I would be telling them things they already knew, from time to time. On the other hand, they agreed to ask me to elaborate, if they needed to know more about a particular process or practice. By the time we were having a drink in the Vaults, I felt as though I was getting to know them.

Next came the meeting with Jock. Afternoon was not a good time to talk to him. I managed to dig him out from a late sitting on the allowance bench. Back in the Vaults, I introduced him to the assembled company and explained to him that they had come to Sheffield to compare the working conditions with those at Castle Eden.

'Conditions? I can tell you about conditions!'

With his rolled down wellies and the peak of his cap over his ear, Jock had switched into oratory mode.

'I know you've had it hard where you come from but when I was a child in the Western Isles, conditions were really bad. Conditions were so bad that we were reduced to eating sea-weed!'

I placed a glass of beer in his hand in the hope that it might deflect him from this line of discussion, but to no avail. He continued to expound his experiences of poverty in his part of the world, during the inter-war years, while the Castle Eden men looked on in stunned silence. Eventually, relief came with the arrival of the Head Brewer. I was able to make my farewells to our visitors and

Castle Eden Brewery - founded in 1826 by John Nimmo, a farmer from Haswell.

leave them all to it.

I had no reason to believe that I would ever see the Castle Eden men again. However, a few weeks later, I learned that one of the brewers from that brewery had unexpectedly given his notice in and was about to take up a post with Vaux Brewery of Sunderland. They were going to be short staffed at Castle Eden and I was asked if I would go up there and help them out for a few weeks. I accepted enthusiastically.

I was not quite sure where Castle Eden was. I knew it was in the north-east and from its name I had half-assumed that it was near Newcastle. It was not even in the same county – Newcastle was in Northumberland and Castle Eden was in Co. Durham. (At my time of life, I can't be bothered with the likes of Tyneside, Teesside and Tyne and Wear etc. I prefer to consider Britain as an ancient patchwork of counties, a concept which has served us well for many centuries.) I was to discover that the beautiful, undulating landscape of Durham together with its majestic county town or rather city, was one of England's best-kept secrets.

In my novel, *The Bubble,* I describe it as follows:

'*Between the Tyne and the Tees lies a quiet land; a place once contested by English, Scot and Norseman, but now their swords sleep with them, beneath the earth. It is a land of small market towns with hovis-cobbled streets and the spires and towers of medieval churches. It is also a land where the ebb-tide of the Industrial Revolution has left the jetsam of industrial hamlets without industry and pit villages without pits. One city stands above this realm, caught in a loop of the River Wear, in a noose of history, a monument to the past. The rest has become forgotten.'*

The village of Castle Eden itself was of such historical interest that it deserved having a book dedicated to it alone. It was rather widely scattered, with the old village and church located about half a mile away from the more populated section, which was known as the Factory. It got this name because of the cotton works erected there by Roland Burdon, who had been elected Member of Parliament for the county of Durham in 1790. He had lived in *Castle Eden House* or *The Castle* as it was known locally, just north-east of the church. Not only was he a leading force in the development of the town of Sunderland but he virtually owned the whole of Castle Eden at that time.

Mention must be made in passing of Castle Eden Dene, which was a unique and beautiful wooded valley that ran from the village down to the sea, some three miles away. When David Bellamy visited it in the 1970s, he observed a plant with the rather incriminating name of, 'Welcome Home Husband However Drunk You Be.'

In 1826, Castle Eden Brewery was founded by John Nimmo, a farmer from Haswell, on property leased from the Burdon family. However, it was known that the first *Castle Eden Inn* on the brewery site was a brewing centre before that. Records show that in the 18th century it was 'a large and commodious inn and posting house... with brewery and malting attached.' The inn was also used as the local court where petty sessions were held for the southern division of Easington Ward. Beginning in 1793, a friendly or benefit society was held at the inn and was said to be the first institution of its kind established in England.

When John Nimmo started brewing at Castle Eden, it seems there were no utilities on the site to speak of and water had to be pumped from six wells in the Dene, a quarter of a mile away. All heavy work had to be done by hand, but later gas was supplied to provide crude mechanical power and to light the buildings. Subsequently, two electricity generators were installed to produce power and light and the brewery provided electric street lighting for Castle Eden. In the days before the Welfare State, Nimmo's ran a free medical service for its employees and provided a golf course and a cricket ground for the village. It is also believed that they were the first brewery in the north to use metal 'corks' for bottles.

In 1867, William Nimmo became the brewery chairman and in 1899, he continued to lease the property which included 50 or 60 acres of farm land. After his death, his ashes were scattered on the brewery site. During my time there, there was still a belief that William Nimmo haunted the brewery and several employees reported seeing a ghostly figure while they were at work. In 1946, the Nimmo family finally bought the brewery buildings and surrounding land, including the golf course, from the Burdon family for the sum of £18,000!

In 1963, Nimmo's became part of the Whitbread group and in 1971, they joined Whitbread East Pennines.

When I arrived at the fine Regency building which was the brewery, I discovered that the interior was as impressive as the stately exterior. The reception area was dominated by an incredibly ornate grandfather clock which dated back to Nimmo's days and looking down upon us all from his framed portrait on the wall, was William Nimmo himself.

I introduced myself and was shown to the production department where I met the Head Brewer and General Manager – Alastair Ross, the Second Brewer – Tony Webb, and the Assistant Brewer – Bill Tarren. Bill was the only staff member who was of true Nimmo vintage. Alastair, I believe, had been transferred there from elsewhere in the Whitbread group and Tony had been Head

Brewer of Tucker's Brewery of Gateshead, which had at some stage been assimilated into Castle Eden Brewery. Bill Tarren, on the other hand, had worked at Castle Eden all his life as had his father before him. He was even more nostalgic and enthusiastic about the brewery in Nimmo's days than I was about the Sheffield brewery in Tennant's days, if that were possible.

Under Nimmo's, the Head Brewer had been Bill Doig. He was well respected and certainly of the 'old school'. Bill Tarren once told me that in his younger days, he had been cleaning in the Tun Rooms (as the fermenting rooms were called at Castle Eden) when Mr Doig had confronted him with the statement, 'Bill, there's been a hop *lurking* under the door mat for three days now.' Nothing else needed to be said.

I learned much about the history and traditions of Castle Eden Brewery from Bill Tarren. Nimmo's draught beers had been renowned in the region – particularly Nimmo's XXXX and Durham Ale. (The convention of designating beers by a number of X's dates back to a time when Excise Officers marked casks of beer with X's to signify that they had been examined and graded for duty. A single X indicated a light or mild ale, XX and XXX were progressively stronger and XXXX was the highest grade.) No less famous were its bottled beers, which included Nimmo's Export Ale (also sold in cans) and Schloss Lager.

It should not be considered surprising that a small north-eastern brewery would be brewing lager. The area was strongly influenced by the brewing practices of Scotland where lager had been brewed since the 19th century. When English brewers from the south started their flirtation with lager brewing in the 1960s and '70s, they were perceived very much as 'Johnnies come lately' by their Caledonian counterparts. Tennent's (spelt with an 'e') Brewery, founded in Glasgow in 1776, had become famous as Scotland's first lager brewery in 1885.

When Whitbread's came into the picture, the Nimmo's products were scrapped and the Head Brewer, with a lifetime of skills and experience to offer, was given 'early retirement'. The old products were replaced by Whitbread Trophy, Best Scotch and Mackeson. The Trophy was brewed in line with the premium draught beers of the regional competitors in that it was stronger than Sheffield Trophy but less bitter – it drank quite 'heavy', which led one of the Castle Eden salesmen to describe it to the press as having 'meat and tatties' in it! Best Scotch was so-named in recognition of the fact that many local competitors brewed Scotch Ales – yet another example of the Scottish influence in the north-east. (At that time, the Head Brewers of the four other breweries in the region were all Scottish.)

Scotch Ales were generally malty and it was said that they were less bitter because they were further away from the hop fields. Scottish bitter beers had names such as Heavy, Special and Export and these names featured strongly amongst the fine choice of premium bitters available to drinkers in the north-east – particularly around the Tyne.

Another set of names for Scottish beers was called the Shilling System, but this was not as prevalent in the north-east. Reflecting perhaps the Scotsman's careful scrutinising of cost, it was based on the 19th century price of beer per barrel; so that 60/- ale was

Nimmo's advert for the draught beer XXXX.

the weakest, 70/- was average strength, 80/- was a premium brew and 90/- was a strong ale. I believe that this traditional method of naming is still carried out on some Caledonian and McEwan beers brewed in Edinburgh, although I presume that they charge 21st century prices over the bar.

Castle Eden Brewery itself, as I have said, was quite small and most of the plant was old. It looked as though very little money had been spent on the place in recent years. However, this was not necessarily to its detriment. 'Many a fine tune is played on an old fiddle,' is as true about brewing as it is about other things and the beer that was produced, albeit Whitbread products, was brewed to the highest standards.

There was an odd selection of fermenting vessels; there were old copper vessels with wooden cladding on them, there were some stainless steel vessels that had once been Yorkshire Squares, but their horizontal decks had been removed so that they became open square

Frank beside the mash-tun at the Castle Eden Brewery.

vessels and there were some very small slate squares of 20 to 30 barrels capacity which in Nimmo's days, had been used for special beers for bottling. Alongside these, rather incongruously, stood a modern, conical bottomed vessel of the type used at Kirkstall.

When the draught beer was run down to the cellar, it was treated in one of three ways. Much of it was racked into cask and supplied the traditional pub trade, but where a particularly long shelf-life was required, such as in the bar of a small sports club that might only be open at weekends or on the other hand, for beer that was supplied to shipping lines, then the beer was filtered and put into keg.

(This is rather reminiscent of the Indian trade in the 19th century. Brewers produced a bottled pale ale of robust strength that was sparkling and well hopped enough to withstand the three months voyage to India where the strong wines and spirits available to the British up until that time, drank rather heavily in such a hot climate. This excellent product became known as India Pale Ale or I.P.A. and is still brewed by some brewers in Britain today.)

However, a significant part of Castle Eden's trade was in Workingmen's or Miners' Clubs where the weekly sales could be as much as a hundred barrels or more. It was clearly not practical to supply this trade with casks or kegs and so bulk processed beer was tankered out to the clubs and delivered into five-barrel tanks in their cellars. Some club cellars looked almost like mini breweries.

Being so isolated from the rest of the group, Castle Eden had to be somewhat self-sufficient. As well as the Engineers department, there was a works department that employed painters, bricklayers, joiners and a painter of inn signs. There was also a small bottling plant and, although it was quite elderly, it was well run and produced good results. Castle Eden Mackeson was bottled on it, together with Guinness that was tankered in from Dublin. Bottled Mackeson was supplied to Scottish and Newcastle Brewery at Newcastle and bulk Mackeson was sent to Federation Brewery also of Newcastle where they bottled it for their own use. (In 1980, Federation moved to a new brewery in Gateshead.) Alongside the bottling plant were the sad, dismantled remains of the small canning plant that had served Nimmo's so well.

There had been a maltings at Castle Eden but this had burnt down some time in the past; in fact it had burnt down twice, in spite of there being a brewery fire brigade!

However, one should not be too critical; brewery maltings quite often burnt down in the past. The combination of dry, dusty conditions and metal parts on malt conveyors and elevators together with friction was a recipe for catastrophe. It just needed one spark. Over the years, some of these fires have entered into brewing folklore, in which brewers have claimed to have used fire damaged malt and produced a new brew of dark ale or stout of amazing quality and popularity. After the second Castle Eden fire, the maltings were not rebuilt but the storage silos that were left were still being used to store malt. Whitbread's purchased all their malt centrally and allocated it to each of its breweries. Head Brewers no longer had the choice.

I later discovered that individual departments in the brewery often had their own shop steward to represent them, irrespective of the size of the department and this explained why Castle Eden had such a disproportionately high number of shop stewards.

In contrast with the production areas, the distribution depart-ment had a large, modern bottled beer store and loading area. This impressive building was referred to, rather dismissively by the production workers, as 'the shed'. There was also a large bonded warehouse for wines and spirits and tobacco and a well-run vehicle repair shop. These two departments, together with 'the shed', were a reflection of the large area served by Castle Eden Brewery.

Many of the men who worked in the brewery came from the small towns and villages that were scattered around the area. These villages had mostly grown up around collieries which in many cases had long since closed down, leaving the area economically depressed with a high level of unemployment. There was a flavour of the '30s about the region, in which many people had very little, but what they had, they were happy to share. This made jobs at the brewery doubly precious and, like Sheffield, there were many cases of several members of the same family working at the brewery; most memorable of these were the Peacock brothers, of which there were four or five, I cannot remember exactly – there seemed to be one around every corner.

In addition to their generosity, the Castle Eden Brewery people also knew how to enjoy themselves. They ran a sports and social club at the brewery which was quite unique. It was not run by the company but by a committee of people who worked at the brewery and, as the Nimmo's Sports and Social Club it retained the name of the brewery's founder. They bought the beer from the company and organized bar staff and musicians who accompanied the many singers who got up to sing, 'from the floor'.

During the weeks I worked there, I thoroughly enjoyed myself; brewing excellent beer on traditional plant by day and drinking it in equally good company by night. When the time finally came for me to return to Sheffield I was very sorry to leave.

8

Castle Eden

Back in Sheffield, I still had Castle Eden on my mind. Tony Webb, the Second Brewer, had told me that he would soon be leaving Castle Eden to take up the position of Head Brewer of Adnam's Sole Bay Brewery, a charming, traditional brewery in Suffolk. There was no mention of who was going to replace him. I let it be known in Sheffield that I would be very interested in the soon-to-be-vacant post and was overjoyed to learn that Harold Burkinshaw, the Head Brewer was thinking along similar lines. In due course, I was officially appointed Second Brewer at Castle Eden.

Before I left Sheffield, I was presented with a beautiful oak coffee table as a leaving present from my friends and colleagues. In addition to this, I was also given some kitchen knives and glasses by Jock McKinnon and the men from the Barm Alley. I was really touched by this unexpected gesture, particularly since the practical nature of these gifts would assist me in setting up home for myself in the north-east.

When I first moved to my new post, I stayed at the *Castle Eden Inn* until I could find a house. This was not the famous 18th century inn of that name – that one had long since disappeared. It was a pub about a mile away from the brewery that had originally been called *The Railway Inn*, but had been renamed to commemorate the original. It had a fine bar which was patronised by the locals and an excellent restaurant attached. My stay there, which subsequently extended to over a year, was therefore very comfortable and I was well looked after by the managers, Jim and Jenny Kellet.

Castle Eden came within the boundaries of the Northern Section of the Incorporated Brewers' Guild. It was one of the smaller sections and it encompassed just five breweries. The largest of these was Scottish and Newcastle Brewery at Newcastle, also at Newcastle was the Northern Clubs' Federation Brewery which had been set up by working men's clubs in 1919. Then there was Vaux Brewery at Sunderland which still used horses and drays to deliver beer around the town and Cameron's Brewery at Hartlepool. Castle Eden was very much the minnow in the pond.

At that time, many members of the northern section believed that the Guild should act more like a trade union and support the rights of individual brewers when they were threatened by the brewing companies. Regrettably, the other sections of the Guild were, by and large, happy to rely on the 'benevolence' of the companies. It was the policy of the Northern Section to elect its officers from each of the five breweries by rotation. The section had a Chairman, Vice Chairman and Hon. Secretary and when I arrived on the scene it was, by coincidence, the turn of Castle Eden to be represented as Hon. Secretary. In due course, I was pleased and proud to be elected to that post.

The duties of the Hon. Sec., besides being treasurer of the section, were to organise meetings, take the minutes and to organise the annual section banquet. I remember one particular meeting to which I had invited a guest speaker from a company that made a good profit out of collecting the spent grains, dropped from brewery mash tuns, and selling them on to farmers as cattle feed.

The meeting was held at Vaux's *Seaburn Hotel* which overlooked the beautiful, sweeping Seaburn Bay on the edge of Sunderland. As I was climbing the majestic staircase to the upstairs room where the meeting was to be held, I met an elderly gentleman coming the other way whose face I seemed to recognise but whose identity I could not place. Later, during the course of the meeting, when the speaker was confessing that it was not only cows that got fat on brewers' grains, I suddenly uttered, much to the surprise of my immediate neighbours, 'Lowry!' It was L. S. Lowry, the Salford painter. I subsequently learned that the distinguished gentleman often came to Seaburn for his holidays and to do some painting along the coast of the north-east. It was also rumoured that he had a lady friend in the area but that was nobody's business but his own.

At the end of each meeting, the section invited the speaker to a meal in the hotel's excellent restaurant, together with as many members who cared to stay behind. It would be remiss of me if I did not mention the Head Brewer of Vaux Brewery, Ian Dickson, who invariably joined us, regaled us with his lively conversation and wit and ensured that there was a constant supply of vintage port at the table out of his own account. It was greatly appreciated although I'm not quite sure how I got home sometimes.

The annual banquet, traditionally held on the first Friday in March, was the social highlight of the section. It was held alternatively at the *Seaburn Hotel*, Sunderland and the *County Hotel*, Newcastle. Organising it involved sorting out a menu, sending out invitations, working out a seating plan and making sure that everyone paid. In our section, the Hon. Sec. also acted as Master of Ceremonies, introducing the Chairman and the guest speakers.

All the section members were invited and the vast majority of them attended – only those who were unfortunate enough to be on duty at their respective breweries were absent. Members were permitted to bring along personal guests – these were usually people with some connection with the industry. On one occasion, I invited Alan Hall, the Excise Officer at Castle Eden, to be my guest. Alan had had a long career in the Excise Service and was known in many of the breweries of the region. He was very strict in his implementation of the regulations but, as I have indicated earlier, the discipline imposed by an Excise Officer was a beneficial contribution to the running of a brewery and Alan had quickly become a very good friend. However, not everyone shared my views and as I was chatting to one of the Newcastle brewers at the banquet, he suddenly spotted Alan and exclaimed to me:

'How did that old fox get in here?'

'Mr Hall is my personal guest,' I replied in a matter-of-fact tone.

'Oh,' replied my brewer friend, rapidly changing his demeanour, 'how nice to see him.'

Alan was, in fact, well aware that he was known in some circles as the 'old fox' and, on the quiet, he was quite proud of the epithet. Many years before, he had officiated at a Scottish whisky distillery and he once told me of an incident concerning a fox that had happened there.

The distillery itself was in a very isolated location. My first day there was a revelation. A large desk had been placed at my disposal in the distillery building. It was like an old style teacher's desk. When I lifted the lid, I found to my surprise, a half pint glass containing a 'very generous' measure of over-proof whisky. I was told that it was an old tradition – 'the Excise-man's allowance'. I was very happy to comply with such a tradition and discovered subsequently that each day that I worked in the distillery, the glass would be mysteriously replenished.

One evening, when I had been working late, I was walking across the broad yard that separated the distillery from the worker's cottages. I saw something ahead of me. At first, I thought it was a dog. I stood and looked more carefully. It was a fox. It stopped about ten yards in front of me and with an almost insolent casualness, it turned and looked at me, straight in the face. We stared at each other for a few seconds – it seemed much longer – and then it loped off in the direction of the manager's house which formed the third side of the yard. I remembered that the manager kept some poultry on the land at the back of his house. He fed them on spent grains and was very proud of them. They were as fat as barrels. I felt that I ought to warn him of the presence of the fox which, in that location, would probably be ravenously hungry. I knocked on the door of the manager's house for some considerable time before there was any response. Eventually, a light came on in an upstairs room and the night-shirted figure of the manager stuck his angry head out of the window.

'Who the hell is that, at this time of night?'

I started to explain that I had met a fox walking across the yard, but was rudely interrupted:

'Get to your bed, you drunken idiot!'

And with that, the window was slammed shut and a few moments later, the light went out.

The next morning, the place was humming with the news that a fox had broken into the manager's poultry house in the early hours. Of the twelve fat geese that had lived there, one had been taken and the remaining eleven had been killed.

Alan was surprisingly philosophical. 'Up until that time, I had never thought very much about foxes but from that day onwards, I have to admit that I have quite a soft spot for that noble creature.'

Whether he was working at Castle Eden Brewery or at any of the other breweries or even down at Tees Port, Alan invariably called in at the brewery at the end of the working day for a drink in *Grufferty's Bar*. This particular 'drinking hole' was a cosy but discrete bar secreted in the depths of the brewery and was

Frank's farewell to Grufferty's Bar and to the man himself, Jimmy Grufferty.

essentially for the benefit of the foremen and supervisors but was also available to honorary members such as brewers and Excise Officers. It was named after Jimmy Grufferty who was the Senior Foreman and in charge of the cellars, a position that enabled him to ensure that the bar was always well stocked. Jimmy was a foreman of the (good) old school. He always addressed me as Mr Priestley and could not bring himself to call me Frank – the practice I had imported from Sheffield – but I respected him for it.

A lot of useful communication took place in *Grufferty's Bar* but mostly it was a place of laughter. People would recount the funny things that had happened during the course of the day such as when George Davies, the Transport Foreman was answering the phones in the Gatehouse. It was a particularly busy day and the internal and external phones had been ringing incessantly. At one stage, he was observed to answer, 'Gatehouse here!' before he had had time to pick up the receiver.

And then there were the jokes. I have never heard or told as many jokes as I did in *Grufferty's Bar*. From time to time, someone would bring in a tin of snuff and although we knew what the result would be, we all eventually were persuaded to start sniffing the stuff. We would each be sneezing uncontrollably and between the explosions, would be laughing at the sneezing of the others.

On one occasion, when we had been on a foremen's night out, we called in to *Grufferty's Bar* for a 'night cap', after the pubs had closed. We were all well and truly 'relaxed'. Jimmy decided to entertain us with a song. Supported (physically) by his colleague Dennis Booth, the Foreman Painter, he burst forth – 'If you ever go across the sea to...' If there had been anyone present who was not already familiar with that beautiful ballad, they would have remained in ignorance of the location, across the sea, that they might have ever gone to. For the song and Jimmy Grufferty, under the influence of emotion and alcohol, faded into silence.

As I mentioned earlier, Castle Eden had a modern, stainless steel, conical bottomed fermenting vessel. I had satisfied myself, years earlier in Sheffield, that the best flavours were obtained by fermenting in shallow, copper FVs and was therefore rather concerned about having to ferment ales in a very deep stainless vessel. I soon discovered that the beer from this vessel did have a slightly harsh flavour to it and, after speaking to Bill Tarren, found that they had been able to get around this problem by blending the conical vessel beer with that from the traditional FVs. As an additional precaution, I made sure that only Mackeson Stout was fermented in the conical vessel from now onwards. Mackeson was a sweet stout which owed its unique flavour to the interesting blend of sugars used in its recipe, rather than to the intricacies of the fermentation process.

Mackeson had been brewed originally at the brewery of Mackeson & Co. of Hythe in Kent, in 1907. However, they became part of the Whitbread Company in 1928. The characteristic flavour of Mackeson was achieved by using a proportion of un-fermentable sugars, including lactose or 'milk sugar' which gave rise to such stouts being known as 'milk stout'. After the war, brewers were discouraged from using the words milk stout as it implied that the drink contained milk. In consequence, Mackeson simply displayed a picture of a milk churn on its label for many years. In the 1950s and 1960s, it was regularly advertised on television and subsequently became the market leader.

We were lucky to have on our staff, not only Bill Tarren who knew the Castle Eden inside out, but also Jack Reddy who was intimately familiar with the Whitbread Company and its products. As Assistant Brewer, Jack had recently come up from the Whitbread headquarters in Chiswell Street, London to take the place of the brewer who had left to join Vaux Brewery. Jack had an incredible sense of humour and was also a very good artist.

Unlike Bill and myself, who had started our careers in breweries that were later taken over, Jack had started his brewery career at

The cooperage quadrangle at the Whitbread Brewery, once the only brewery within the city of London.

Whitbread's, but not just Whitbread's, he had started at the famous, old Whitbread Brewery on Chiswell Street in the City of London – at that time, the only brewery in the City of London. And while I had some reservations about the company that had superseded the traditions of the brewery that had appointed me, Jack quite rightly and understandably had a great deal of affection and respect for the parent company.

Whitbread & Co. had been founded in 1742 by Samuel Whitbread (1720-1796), the son of a Bedfordshire farmer. At the age of fourteen, he had been sent to London by his widowed mother to be an apprentice brewer. Eight years later, he established himself as a brewer in his own right at premises on Whitecross Street in Finsbury and in 1750, he bought the little King's Head Brewery on Chiswell Street, which he progressively developed and enlarged.

It was said that his success was due, not only to his personal standards of excellence in the quality of his beer, but his continual work to improve the efficiency of the plant brewing it. In this context, he was skilful in engaging the interest of some of the foremost engineers and scientists of the day.

John Smeaton, chiefly known perhaps for rebuilding Eddystone lighthouse, designed six underground beer storage cisterns, the largest of which had a capacity of 3,600 barrels. John Rennie, who had designed London, Southwark and Waterloo bridges, supervised the introduction of steam power into the brewery in 1775.

The steam engine, which was designed by James Watt, was one of his biggest. It was a 70hp machine and was used for raising brewing liquor and for grinding the malt. It was one of the wonders of London and in 1787, King George III, Queen Charlotte and other members of the royal family visited the brewery to see for themselves the great stone cisterns and Watt's 'stupendous Steam Engine'.

Not surprisingly, by the end of his life, Samuel Whitbread's brewery was producing 202,006 barrels of porter a year (ale was not brewed there until 1834), making it the leader amongst the twelve main London breweries at that time.

In 1871, the French scientist, Louis Pasteur visited the brewery. He spent some time studying beer fermentations as part of his research into better production. At his suggestion, the brewery acquired a microscope for the purpose of examining yeast. It has been said that this event sowed the seeds for the company's research and control laboratories. The microscope was still in good working order and on display in Chiswell Street City Cellars over a hundred years later.

Even Whitbread's prize-winning shire horses, which were used for beer deliveries around the City, were steeped in tradition. Viscount Eversley, who was married to the daughter of Samuel Whitbread II and was a partner in the company, was elected Speaker of the House of Commons in 1839.

Following this event, Whitbread horses were used to pull the Speaker's coach on special state occasions, including the Corona-tions of King Edward VII, King George V, King George VI and at that of the present Queen in 1953. Three pairs of brewery shires were also used to draw the new Lord Mayor's coach and could be seen in London on Lord Mayor's Day in November.

With traditions such as these, I was tempted to look more sympathetically upon our parent company. Sadly, this enthusiasm was destined to be short-lived. However, for the time being, I was more occupied with the present than the past.

Alastair Ross, the Head Brewer and General Manager gave us the news one day that he was leaving the company to take up a post at Samuel Smith's Old Brewery in Tadcaster. I remember at the time that I was quite surprised that he would wish to relinquish such an attractive post at Castle Eden. The new Head Brewer and General Manager was Brian Spencer who I already knew from Sheffield. He had been First Assistant Brewer (FAB) there for a short time before I moved north. In his new post, he told me that he wanted to concentrate on the General Manager aspect of his job, leaving me to do most of the brewing – an arrangement with which I was very happy.

It was around this time that I bade farewell to the *Castle Eden Inn* and finally moved into my new house in Elwick. This rural village had a large picturesque green around which were spaced some attractive houses and cottages, a shop, a post office and two inviting public houses. The first one, *The Spotted Cow*, was a Cameron's house but the second, *The McOrville*, was a Castle Eden house and had been named after a stud horse. Elwick with its two pubs was like a town that had two football teams – you either supported one or the other, but not both. Naturally, I was a McOrville man. Some of the older customers there suggested rather uncharitably, that *The Spotted Cow* had got its name from the type of lady who patronised it.

The licensee of *The McOrville* was Ronnie Warrand; his family had run the pub for many years. It had a pleasant lounge which was generally used by newcomers, a small bar which was usually packed shoulder to shoulder with local regulars and a connecting corridor where those who wished to drink after hours lurked. The actor Ian Hendry, the original 'Avenger', used to call in to the lounge occasionally, on his way back from Newcastle. The popularity of the pub was largely due to Ronnie's outrageous repartee. If I ever went in wearing a suit (which was not very often), he would hurl the Spoonerism loudly across the bar, 'My, you're a fart smeller!' much to everyone's amusement.

On another occasion, when I was not wearing a suit, I had just got in the door when he called across the crowd, 'I've heard what you've been doing this afternoon. Did it make your bottom sore?' The activity he was referring to, I must explain, was riding a bicycle. Generous lunches in the brewery canteen and steak house dinners in the *Castle Eden Inn* together with the odd pint of ale throughout the days and evenings had led to my putting on weight for the first time in my life. I had decided therefore, to remedy the situation by some additional physical activity.

I had bought the bike by mail order because it was cheap. When it was delivered, I could see why. Shortly after Ronnie's exposé, it exploded – or so it seemed. I was riding down a steep hill and as I began to pick up speed, I applied the brakes. As the brake blocks engaged against the rim of the front wheel, one of them suddenly shot out like a bullet. The clamp that had been holding the block dug into the wall of the tyre, tearing a hole in it and the inner tube, no longer restrained by the tyre, bulged out through the hole. I watched helplessly as the tube ballooned out to the size of a football and then burst very loudly. This incident marked the end of my enthusiasm for cycling.

After I had moved into my new house, I received a surprise gift from someone at the brewery. It was a hand painted house sign which had been made and was given to me by Harry Bartlett, the Foreman Signwriter at Castle Eden. Harry, who had forty years service with the company, painted all the pub signs for the brewery. He had appeared on Tyne-Tees Television in a programme devoted to the more unusual types of occupation. I remember that he was meticulous in his painting of inn signs that depicted coats of arms, of which there were many in the region.

Historically, in the dim and distant past, when most people could neither read nor write, people used signs to denote their occupation. Thus in Roman times, the sign of a goat might have denoted a dairy, whereas a mule driving a mill may have indicated a miller or baker. Roman wine purveyors advertised their trade with a bunch of vine leaves or ivy and similarly, early English ale-sellers were required by law to display an ale-stake or pole to show that they brewed ale for sale and as we have seen earlier, the pole would be decorated with some greenery when their wares had been approved by the ale conner. This may have been a distant echo of some of the inn signs that we can still see today, such as *The Ivy, The Bush, The Holly Bush* and other examples of trees and greenery. As literacy became more widespread, the practice of displaying trade signs began to decline; the main exception was for inns and taverns. I am not sure what this says about the intellectual capacity of the patrons of such establishments.

By the 17th century, many ale sellers were getting more adventurous with their signs. Carved and painted effigies of birds or animals were hung from their ale stakes in a hoop. Swans, hens and cocks were common and it is believed that the sign of a cock in a hoop gave rise to the expression 'cock-a-hoop'. Thereafter, it was a short step from a painted carving to a painted signboard. These boards were either suspended from the front of the house or from a post located in front of the premises. It seems that alehouse keepers were keen to outdo each other on the size of their signboards and some of these extended all the way across the street, forming an archway. Over the centuries, laws were passed in an attempt to curtail these structures but clearly not everyone paid heed and some examples can still be seen today.

The largest and most ornate sign of this type was erected at the *White Hart Inn* at Scole in Norfolk in 1655. Amongst the many carvings that adorned it were representations of the goddess Diana, Father Time, Neptune astride a dolphin and Jonah emerging from the mouth of a whale. Hanging from the centre of the arch was a white hart surrounded by a wreath. It was said to have cost over a thousand pounds; a fortune in Tudor times. Sadly, by the 19th century, it was becoming a danger to traffic and eventually it had to be dismantled. It is not clear what happened to it thereafter.

With the emergence of signboards, the variety of inn names proliferated. John Bickerdyke, author of *The Curiosities of Ale & Beer,* wrote of these early days: 'If mine host were a man of small imagination, he might still be content with a bush or with the arms of some local magnate, but if he were a man of fancy, his imagination, in quest of a worthy sign, might revel unrestrained through the highways and byways of history ancient and modern, political and natural.' In other words, there emerged an enormous diversity of inn signs which is still evident today. Examples range from the *Saracen's Head* which harks back to the time of the crusades, to the *Silent Woman,* who was depicted without a head at all. However, not all signs were of equal artistic merit. It is believed that the 'grinning Cheshire cat' originated from a rather amateur portrayal of a Lion Rampant by a sign painter of that county.

Living away from Castle Eden and the brewery, I began to explore the surrounding villages in my quest for interesting 'drinking holes'. One of my favourite was the *Red Lion* at Trimdon Village – a pub that regularly hosted live music. In the middle of the week, an excellent group called *The Country Gentlemen* used to perform country music or, as it was known then, country and western music. On Friday night, I think it was, it was Folk Club night. The resident performers were a remarkable group called *Skerne,* named after a small river that flowed nearby. I can still recall their lusty rendition of 'On the Banks of the Roses'.

A few years later, the leader of the group, John Burton, would often introduce us to a young man in a suit who sometimes arrived late and stood at the back of the room, against the bar. It was Tony

Blair – he had been elected M.P. for the Sedgefield ward in 1983. John Burton became his constituency agent.

One of the most sociable groups of men at Castle Eden was 'Dad's Army'. They had nothing to do with the television programme of that name – they were a group of ex-servicemen, most of whom had seen active service, who raised hundreds of pounds every year for charitable causes such as outings for local, disadvantaged children and medical research. Dad's Army was a splinter group of the Nimmo's Sports and Social Club and the founders, who worked in various departments of the brewery, included Jack Harland, Jimmy Bell, Bill O'Brien, Harry Prescott, Alan Richardson and Billy Cooper, who was the oldest member.

There were about forty members and I was surprised and pleased when they asked me to join them as an honorary member – surprised because I had never served in the armed forces, I had not even been required to do National Service – and pleased because these men were excellent company and drinking companions. They held a social evening on the first Tuesday of each month

Dad's Army on a march to raise money for the
Lesley Scott Memorial Appeal.

in the Social Club. There was no shortage of singers from 'the floor' and there was always an organist or accordionist on hand to accompany the 'artists'. In addition to this, there were recitations, including Bill O'Brien's much requested rendition concerning the amorous adventures of 'The Village Blacksmith'.

Dad's Army were able to raise cash in a variety of ways. One year, two of the draymen, Jim Evans and Eric Wilson raised over five hundred pounds delivering beer around the pubs of the north-east, dressed as Batman and Robin. However, the main fundraising event was the annual sponsored walk. This was carried out on Easter Monday and involved a hike of around 15 or 20 miles around the local villages, calling in at all the Castle Eden pubs and clubs along the way, including the Ex-servicemen's Club.

I took part in most of the walks while I was at Castle Eden and was not a little concerned to discover that there were at least twelve stops on the way and we had a pint at each of them – usually donated free by the publican. Each of us was sponsored by friends and colleagues to complete the course and in addition to this; money was collected from the customers of the various establishments that we visited. I remember that our first stop was at *The Mason's Arms* in Easington, a very traditional pub, run by Mrs Bella Coxon, a lovely lady. She maintained several old customs such as handing out paste eggs to her regulars at Easter and the main bar as a strictly a men-only area. However, by the time I had completed the walk, my memories of individual locations were less clear.

The walk finished at the brewery Social Club where a crowd of employees had collected to welcome us back and to join in the party that had been organised there. An abundance of food and drink was laid on as well as entertainment – one year the guitarist Bert Weedon was invited. My natural reserve being weakened by exhaustion and alcohol, it was not unusual for me to finish the evening in the arms of a lovely, soft, warm woman, of which there were many in the north-east. What a terrible life!

During my time at Castle Eden, the most senior member of

Billy Cooper, the most senior member of Dad's Army

Dad's Army, Billy Cooper, was due to retire. He had started at the brewery in the 1920s as a bricklayer/mason but had left some years later to join the regular army, only to return at the end of the war in 1945. On his last day at the brewery, Brian Spencer, the General Manager, presented him with a radio/cassette player and Bill, after thanking his friends for their generosity, made the following observation, 'When Mr Nimmo set me on in 1924, he never said anything about it being only temporary!'

⊂◯⊃

Another and even more arduous walk that I got involved in was the Lyke Wake Walk, which stretched across the North Yorkshire Moors for around forty miles. The route, which started in Osmotherley in the west and concluded at Ravenscar on the coast, was in some way associated with the journey, in ancient times, of the dead to their final resting place. Lyke-wake was the watch kept over a dead body. In medieval times, coffins containing the dead sometimes had to be carried great distances in search of consecrated ground in which they could be buried.

The expeditions, which were carried out on three consecutive summers, were organised by a group of men from the brewery garage, in particular, George Bean and Dougie Foster. We usually set off from Osmotherley at 8pm on Friday evening with the aim of reaching the coast by mid morning Saturday. The walk had to be completed in under 24 hours to be valid. It was a particular credit to our walkers that we were able to complete this overnight hike after a full day's work and after consuming our 'normal daily allowance' of beer.

There were several roads criss-crossing the moor and whenever we reached one we would be met by Dougie in the minibus dispensing encouragement and refreshments. At first, a glass of beer and a sandwich was all we needed but later, when it was dark, we were pleased to discover that Dougie had prepared a large pan full of hot, nourishing soup. It was thick and creamy with crunchy strips of onion in it. He had heated it up on a camping stove, illuminated by a portable lamp. It was greatly appreciated, particularly as there was enough of it to last for several stops.

When it had all gone, Dougie asked if we had all enjoyed it. We agreed that we had. He went on to explain rather guiltily that he could now tell us the truth. When he was heating up the soup, a large moth had flown into it, attracted by the light of the lamp. He had tried to extricate it with the ladle but only succeeded in pushing it deeper in. He had therefore stirred it in with the rest and since the soup had been consumed entirely, it was clear that one of us must have eaten a moth! Happily, we were far too weary to worry about it.

Later, when I was even more tired, we made a stop at a place where a group of Territorial Army soldiers were having a break. We had seen them several times that night – they must have been following the same route as us. It was quite light now and George and I were sitting on a rock watching a rather shapely female soldier stretching up to reach something out of the back of their lorry. 'Nice arse,' I observed to George. I was quite surprised when the young lady turned round and looked at me with a rather embarrassed smile.

Stupefied by exhaustion, I had not realised that I was speaking in a normal voice and that the lovely soldier was only a few yards away.

Eventually, we managed to drag our aching bodies into Ravenscar. George registered our accomplishment at the Post Office shop and a few weeks later, we received our Lyke Wake Walk ties. They were black and covered in coffins – an appropriate reflection of our condition at the end of that gruelling expedition.

━●━

At Castle Eden, the men's beer allowance was served in a bar that was situated in the modern building, which housed the Social Club and the Canteen. The bar was known by all as the 'Wet Canteen'. I used to enjoy calling in there at 5pm on Fridays for a drink and a laugh with the men. As they used to say round there, the 'crack' was always good.

The assistant brewers and I used to share the duty of checking the brewery during the night. When it was my turn, I used to call in around 10pm. The first job was to check that all the excise entries were up to date in the book and then I would go and have a look at the fermentations. A brew might need an extra rousing to speed it up or, on the other hand, cooling to slow it down. The relevant instructions would then be passed on to the Tun Room operative. If the man happened to Billy Shut, who at that time would be hosing down the floors before the night shift came on; caution would have to be exercised in relaying the message. When hearing a voice behind him, Billy had the habit of swinging round, maintaining the hose-pipe in a horizontal position, soaking the speaker from head to foot. I would rather be wet on the inside than on the outside.

The night shift came on at 11pm and after messages had been

exchanged and the state of the brewery assessed, they would often join me in the Wet Canteen for a 'night-cap'. We were often joined by the shift boiler man. Since the boiler worked largely automatically, this man had other duties, including the responsibility for the general security of the site. So much so, that one of the boiler men liked to be known as 'Security'. This sometimes led to the remark being made, 'I see that 'Security' is tight tonight'.

The Wet Canteen was in sight of the road that passed the brewery and consequently, drinking had to be conducted in the dark. A light would have attracted amateur drinkers and other unwanted passing types, like moths to a candle. One repercussion of this was that courting couples, assuming the building to be unoccupied, would park their cars in the car park alongside the windows and perform their passionate gymnastics in full view of the concealed and largely indifferent imbibers. Fortunately, I never witnessed such an exhibition; I feel sure it would have detracted from my enjoyment of the ale.

I remember one particular winter evening when it had been snowing steadily since lunch time. I was worried about the night shift being able to get in and so I was greatly relieved when they all arrived on time. Later, when we walked up to the Wet Canteen, the wind was blowing the snow almost horizontally and it seemed to be deepening by the minute. Things were looking black – or rather white!

We were onto our second pint when we suddenly heard an alarm bell ringing. 'That'll be the Wines and Spirits,' said 'Security'. 'It's probably been set off by the wind.' I accompanied him out into the blizzard after telling the men, 'I may be some time,' and we followed the sound of the alarm down to the Wines and Spirits warehouse. The doors were secure and we could find no sign of intruder's footprints in the snow. However, the building would have to be checked and the alarm re-set. The only key holder was the Wines and Spirits Supervisor, Mrs Grace Evans who lived in the nearby village of Hesleden. We telephoned her and she told us that she was quite willing to come out but she would need transport.

And so, with two of the 'heaviest' men in the back seat of my car (for ballast and in case we needed a push), we set off for Hesleden. The main road, in front of the brewery, was not too bad but when we turned left down the road to the coast, we found that the snow had been drifting alarmingly between the hedges on either side. The snow was falling so thickly that the men in the back could see nothing through their windows. They were stunned into silence by their isolation from any familiar landmarks. My view out of the front windscreen was not much better. I was thinking to myself that I must keep the car moving; if I had to stop in these conditions, I would never get it going again.

Unbeknown to me, a little way ahead, a large part of a tree had been blown down, blocking most of the road. By the time I saw it in the beam of the lights, it was too late to think. I swerved left, round the end of the tree, mounting a bank of snow which concealed the pavement. Having miraculously by-passed one obstacle, I found myself confronted by an abandoned vehicle. I swerved right to avoid the car, maintaining a 'decent speed' all the while and narrowly missed the wall on that side of the road. I then swerved left again to get back into the middle of the road but was then aware that the back end of the car was sliding to the right. I instinctively steered into it and, as if by magic, the car corrected itself and we continued along the road. For a few moments, not a word was spoken, after which, a voice from the back piped up, 'Not much chance of getting constipated in this bloody car.'

We arrived at Grace's house without further incident and on the return journey, I was not looking forward to encountering the fallen tree again. As we approached, my spirits sunk deeper. There were flashing blue lights; the police had arrived. One of their number, who my passengers informed me was PC W–, was attempting to pull the tree clear while most of his colleagues stood by and watched him. We were flagged down to stop and I warned the men to try and look sober. I wound the window down and explained our mission to the bending officer, trying to avoid breathing alcoholic fumes into his face. By this time, part of the road had been cleared and they waved us on. However, as predicted, the tyres would not grip on the freshly compacted snow and we were stuck. The officer then motioned to the standing constables who, shoulders pushing and feet slipping, gave the car enough speed to continue on its merry way.

As I drove back towards the brewery, I could not help smiling to myself at the scene I had just witnessed – four cold and wet policemen pushing a car whose passengers included three 'beery' men, back to a brewery.

By this time, the storm had abated and it had stopped snowing. When we arrived back, Grace and I, together with 'Security', wandered down to the warehouse where the alarm was still ringing loudly – loud enough to drive men to drink, in fact. Grace checked the stock and found that all was well. She re-set the alarm and locked up and we strolled back to the Wet Canteen. I was ready for a drink. When we walked through the door, an unexpected sight met us. Most, if not all of the police we had met earlier were thoroughly enjoying our hospitality. They said that they had just called in to make sure that everything was alright. I assured them that it was but that they were very welcome to have a drink with us. This invitation was purely academic since the brewery lads had already ensured that every policeman was in possession of a full glass of ale.

Two of the police said they would take Grace back to Hesleden – an offer I quickly accepted. I did not fancy driving down that road again that night. After draining their glasses, they were off, but after their mission had been accomplished, they returned to rejoin the party. At first, I felt slightly uneasy at the sight of the local constabulary enjoying the hospitality of this hitherto exclusive retreat, but as the ale flowed fast and free, these doubts were mostly washed away. Eventually, as we drank into the early hours and the party showed no sign of breaking up, I made my excuses and left, in the sure knowledge that I would not be encountering any police on the road that night.

After the storm incident, the police became occasional but regular nocturnal visitors to the Wet Canteen; none more regular than PC W–, who was known to some of the brewery men. He was known as 'W–, the Hero' because of a story going round that he had saved an old lady from a house fire. Some of his colleagues reported that the 'fire' was little more than a fall of soot but this could have been prompted by professional jealousy. I was prepared to give him the benefit of the doubt, as we meet far too few heroes in this life. He was an amiable type and any man who appreciates fine ale, certainly has something to commend him.

On one occasion when he was drinking with us in the Wet Canteen, he seemed uncharacteristically anxious. A new Sergeant had been transferred to their station who was shaking things up a bit in that quiet backwater. It was a case of 'new brooms sweeping clean.' After a few drinks, W–, the Hero, began to relax until suddenly the air was filled with a totally unfamiliar voice. 'Control to PC W–. Please state your position.'

'Your left tit just spoke,' I observed to a petrified W–. He grasped his chest as though he was about to have a heart attack and retrieved the offending two-way radio from his breast pocket. At the same time, it was noticed that a police patrol car was driving slowly along the road outside the brewery.

'Bleedin 'ell! It's the new sarge,' he gasped, as he dived frantically onto the floor to avoid detection. The radio again spoke out.

'Control to PC W–. Please state your position. I repeat – please state your position.'

W–, the Hero, raised the radio to his lips but fear and indecision prevented him from uttering any words into it. Eventually the patrol car passed by and after a safe interval, PC W– beat a hasty retreat. He ran to his car, which he had concealed behind the canteen and screeched onto the public highway, from which location he could legitimately answer any further calls that might be directed at him.

We received no further visits from the police for several days, but a week or so later we learned that it was PC W—'s colleagues who had played the trick on him. Assuming that he would be in the Wet Canteen, they had driven past the brewery and made the calls. It was not a very gentlemanly act to disturb a man's enjoyment of his beer – particularly when that man was a 'hero'.

On another occasion, when I was drinking with one of the other Tun Room shifts, the remains of a keg of lager was discovered in the Wet Canteen. It had probably been left over from one of the day-time trade parties. Now lager is not my cup of tea and to be honest, in those days, even a cup of tea was not my cup of tea. But one of the shift men, who I shall call 'Kevin', was very partial to lager, in spite of the fact that to me, it was almost tasteless and over-carbonated. The effect that this gassy brew had on Kevin was that it caused him to break wind quite frequently. It is an established fact that all drinkers break wind from time to time, as do the rest of the population, but Kevin's 'outbursts' were more numerous than was the average. Not only that, but by cautious control of the relevant muscles he had the ability to modulate the pitch of his 'wind instrument'. In other words, he could fart tunefully.

On this particular night, he had been giving us the benefit of his unique aptitude when his repertoire was mercifully cut short. We were about to receive visitors. A police car had been seen snaking its way behind the building. When they entered the bar, I was pleased to see that WPC G— was with them. WPC G— was a very attractive police woman but sadly she did not visit us as frequently as her male colleagues. While the men were happy to stand around the bar, WPC G— hitched herself up onto a bar stool, revealing a generous expanse of thigh, enough to hold the attention of every man in the room.

'Actually, you've just missed a treat,' I said innocently, 'Kevin has been giving us a lovely tune.'

'Leave off,' muttered Kevin, under his breath.

'Oh, I didn't know you were a singer, Kevin,' cooed WPC G—,

unaware of his special 'gift'. 'Will you start the song again for me?'

'No I can't, really.' Kevin was now red with embarrassment.

'He's got a remarkable voice,' I said, winding up the pressure.

'Oh come on Kevin,' implored WPC G—, smiling at him sweetly. 'You start, and I'll join in.'

After that last remark, we could no longer hold back the flood gates of laughter, much to the confusion of our guests, who could merely smile and speculate.

It was not the only time when the police were 'in the dark'. There was the story of the owl which perched on a large tree across from the brewery. Illuminated by the street light, it could be seen from the windows of the Wet Canteen. The shift men (Bob Darby in particular) used to point it out to the visiting policemen. The conversation would start with, 'I see the owl's out tonight,' and the police would seek it out, find it, admire it and even discuss it at their leisure, over foaming pints. The truth was that there was no owl. There never had been. There was just an old broken branch which caught the light in a particular way. The brewery men knew it and I knew it but to this day, I have no idea whether our guests ever discovered the joke.

From time to time at Castle Eden, I had the pleasure of escorting parties of visitors around the brewery, as I had done in Sheffield. One particular party that I remember, consisted of a group of Trade Union officials from one of the emerging black African countries. The trip had been arranged by the British Trades Union movement and several of our own shop stewards accompanied the tour. When we had reached the Tun Rooms, we all peered over the edge of a vessel, watching a slightly embarrassed man cleaning it.

'How much money would a man earn, doing this job?' asked one of our guests. I told him the amount and he seemed quite impressed and as he discussed it with his colleagues, it was clear from what they were saying that they believed that the sum mentioned was a monthly wage rather than a week's wage. I quickly put them right and they told me in astonishment that such a weekly wage was much more than they would earn in a month, back home. I nudged our brewery shop steward who was standing beside me and said, as seriously as I could, 'I've always thought we were paying you lot too much.' Fortunately, even shop stewards have a sense of humour.

On another occasion, I again had a party of Trade Union officials, but this time they were from Czechoslovakia (as it was known then). The officials themselves were rather subdued; they had visited one of the Newcastle breweries the day before and they were still suffering from the after effects of legendary Geordie hospitality. However, their interpreter was a charming lady called Hana. She was in fine form and was telling me about the renowned brewing industry of her native land and of the many special beers that they brewed there. (The word 'pilsner', for instance, related to beer brewed in the Czechoslovakian town of Pilsen.)

By a fortunate chance, I found a case of Gold Label Barley Wine behind the bar and was pleased to introduce her to that 'special brew'. She took to it immediately and by the time we were on our second or third, she had started calling them 'Golden Angels', which I thought was a perceptive and appropriate description.

After a while, she asked me if I had ever visited Czechoslovakia. 'Many times,' I replied expansively. She was taken aback by my effusive answer, since her country was not, at that time, one of the major locations on the tourist map. I felt I needed to explain.

Some years before, I had taken a two week holiday in neighbouring Poland. I had spent the first week in Warsaw and Krakow and the second week in the southern town of Zakopany. From there, I had taken a trip to the Tatra range of mountains which formed a natural boundary between Poland and Czechoslovakia. I was told that there was a family of wild bears living in the region, that crossed backwards and forwards over the border at will. The Poles claimed that they were Polish bears and the

Czechs claimed they were theirs. As I scanned the ridge which formed the frontier, I could see that large stones had been placed along it at intervals, with the colours of the Polish flag painted on one side and the Czechoslovakian colours painted on the other. Tourists such as I were not supposed to stray onto the Czechoslovakian side, since we did not have the relevant papers and visas. However, fortified by the local plum brandy, I strolled along the ridge, stepping first on one side and then on the other, chanting to myself, 'Poland, Czechoslovakia, Poland...etc.' So it was, that I had visited Czechoslovakia 'many times'.

Although our Trade Union guests revived only a little from their hangovers, Hana and I had a thoroughly enjoyable session and a week or so later, she sent me a post card from Prague saying that she still could not forget the taste of 'Golden Angels'.

Many years later, I heard a story which strangely complemented my recollections of Hana and the 'Golden Angels'. I had been visiting Dalwhinnie Whisky distillery in the Highlands, which at over a thousand feet above sea level, was one of the highest distilleries in the land. The guide told me that he had taken a party of Czechoslovakians around the distillery a few years before and he well remembered that one of the party was an attractive young lady wearing hot pants (which should enable a rough date to be put on the story).

Towards the end of the tour, he was explaining the process of maturation, in which the newly-made spirit was filled into oak casks and allowed to stand for several years, during which time the character of the whisky developed and the flavour generally became smoother. An unfortunate consequence of this process was that about two per cent of the whisky evaporated from the casks each year. This loss of whisky into the atmosphere was traditionally known as the 'angel's share'.

The hot pant-ed young lady from the land of saintly King Wenceslas, was too young to have known any regime other than the atheist, Marxist government that was imposed after the war. Consequently, she did not understand what an angel was. There was apparently some difficulty in trying to explain this phenomenon to her. However, I feel sure that the state of confusion would have been amicably settled when they received their complimentary glass at the end of the tour and enjoyed the wonderful experience of Dalwhinnie Malt.

Back in the brewery, it was clear that our old hopback had just about reached the end of its useful life. The hopback (it should be remembered) was the vessel where the spent hops were separated from the wort after boiling. At that time, we were increasingly using hops that had been ground into a powder, to improve utilisation and so it was decided by the powers-that-be that the hopback should be replaced by a more up-to-date (and cheaper) Whirlpool separator. The company would not be buying us one off the shelf; our own Chief Engineer, Bob Butler was given the task of designing one for us.

A Whirlpool separator was a flat-bottomed cylindrical vessel into which wort was pumped at a tangent. This caused the contents to revolve around the tank in the form of a whirlpool which continued after the tank was full. The spent hops and other solids such as protein, collected as a compact conical heap in the centre of the floor of the tank and the clear wort was withdrawn through a pipe at the periphery of the base. That was the theory; a lot of things could go wrong. The tangential inlet had to be at the right level and at the correct angle and the wort had to be pumped in at a rate which resulted in a rotation around the tank of between three and six revolutions per minute. If there were problems with any of these features, the resultant turbulence could well have prevented effective separation from taking place.

It was a tense moment when the time came to put the first brew through the new Whirlpool. We need not have worried. It worked perfectly and continued to do so throughout the time I was

The residue left behind in the Whirlpool Separator after the first trial.

at Castle Eden. Total credit should and did go to Bob Butler, the modest and unassuming Chief Engineer.

I was writing quite a lot of poetry at the time and ironically, some of the best was written while under the influence of hangovers. I am a person who suffers diabolical hangovers, but I do not complain. That is not strictly true. I do complain when I am suffering, but I do not complain that I am subject to such torture. For one who enjoys drinking so much, a hangover is a timely warning. It is Mother Nature's way of saying, 'Take a break.' One such poem is this:

'NEVER AGAIN', AGAIN

'Never again', is easy to say
in the painful morning after.
Forgotten the night of drunken delight,
lechery, liquor and laughter.
With bosoms and bottoms as warm as the smiles
that promised the rise and the fall.
The spirit was willing, but flesh was weak;
thus alcohol sanctifies all.

'Never again', is easy to swear
when your eyeballs threaten to burst,
When your brain cells are burnt and your lessons are learnt
and your laughing-box tastes of the worst.
But what of tomorrow, when your body is well
and the tune starts to run through your brain,
When you're itching to fly and your throat's feeling dry,
will you do it all over again?

This was one of my favourite poems at the time and indeed, others must have shared my enthusiasm because I managed to get it published both in Britain and in the U.S.A.

9

Storm Brewing

While I was at Castle Eden, the two men who had been most instrumental in the development of my career retired. Eric Wiles who, as Chief Chemist at Sheffield, had appointed me as Laboratory Assistant in 1959, retired from his post as Whitbread East Pennines Quality Control Manager after 32 years service at Exchange Brewery, Sheffield. The time I had served in the laboratories had given me the chance to gain a sound understanding of the science of brewing. Harold Burkinshaw had retired from his post as Production Director of Whitbread East Pennines after more than 46 years. It was he who, as the Head Brewer at Sheffield, had provided me with the opportunities, over the years, to learn and understand the art of brewing. He was succeeded by David Barnard, who had previously been Head Brewer at Whitbread's modern brewery at Luton.

The policy of internal promotion was becoming eroded. When key personnel retired, who had started their careers in the independent breweries that had been subsequently swallowed up by Whitbread, they were being replaced by Whitbread's own men.

However, I was not too concerned at this stage. I was enjoying life in and out of the brewery and, still being single, I could afford holidays abroad. My favourite locations were in Central Europe but I also enjoyed visiting Belgium, which was a major brewing country at that time and still regularly brews over 450 different varieties of beer today.

I recently revisited that civilised country and spent much of my time carrying out 'consumer research' in the old Flemish town of Bruges where just one brewery still survives. It is known locally as Heavy Henry – a name that applies, it seems, not only to the beer brewed there but also to the owner of the establishment. The brewery has been in the same family for many years and therefore it has been necessary to name the first-born son of each generation 'Henry' in order to maintain the tradition. It was not reported however, how each successive Henry managed to maintain his 'heaviness'. I venture to suggest that they achieved this by enjoying the fruits of their labour as much as I did.

In another part of the town, I came upon a lane with the curious name of 'Blind Donkey'. It had once boasted a tavern with the reputation of selling the cheapest beer in town. As a result, it was the most popular of the many drinking holes in Bruges. At closing time, it was the unsteady and shoulder-scuffing progress of its patrons along this narrow thoroughfare that had given rise to its otherwise inexplicable title.

It was just as well that these exotic visits relaxed and rejuvenated me because on returning to Castle Eden, I sometimes found interesting and unusual problems waiting for me.

On one occasion, I returned from distant shores to a brewery full of cloudy beer. The fermentations were uncharacteristically sluggish, the traditional draught beer would not settle out and clarify after fining in the cellar and the beer that was required for kegs and tanks just blocked the filters up and brought them to a standstill. We quickly established that the wort in the fermenting vessels was thick with protein haze. This was slowing down the fermentation process and preventing the beer from clearing in the cellars. Finings facilitated yeast separation by an electrostatic mechanism. Yeast cells were negatively charged and so repelled each other and tended to remain in suspension. Isinglass finings on the other hand consisted of positively charged particles which attracted large numbers of yeast cells to form a clump. When these clumps of yeast reached a certain size and weight, they sunk to the bottom of the cask, leaving the beer clear and bright.

On this occasion, the yeast cells had been 'smothered' by protein particles, preventing them from interacting with the finings and inhibiting any clarification. Similarly with the keg and tank beer, after only a few barrels had passed through the filter, the pads became blocked with protein and the process came to a halt. The lengthy task of dismantling the filter, cleaning it out, repacking it and sterilising it had to be repeated time and again, day and night, to satisfy the demands of the trade.

It turned out that the malt we were using and that had been dispatched to us by Central Purchasing had a very high protein content – so high, that normally it would have been considered unsuitable for brewing. The Group Research and Development department that analysed all materials purchased, had not alerted us to this fact.

I subsequently discovered that during the growing period of this new season's malt the weather had been particularly dry and consequently, the individual barley corns were smaller than usual. This was reflected in a smaller than usual percentage of starchy material in the interior of the corns, which meant that the percentage of protein material was higher. This had led to all our problems.

It was clear that the protein would have to be removed from the wort before it reached the fermenting vessel. After consulting Bill Tarren, the Assistant Brewer who had a lifetime's experience with this brewery plant, we agreed that the answer lay at the boiling stage. I immediately instructed the copper-man to extend the boiling time by fifteen minutes and to make sure that the boils were vigorous, in the hope that the protein would be precipitated and removed before fermentation.

Exactly one week later, I felt rather apprehensive as I strode down to the Sample Room to find out whether the first of the 'extra-boiled' brews had clarified after fining. After drawing off the usual couple of cloudy glasses containing the yeast that had settled around the tap, the beer ran clear and sparkling, much to everyone's relief. Several months after this event, a memorandum was sent around the Group from the Research and Development department, to the effect that if any breweries were experiencing problems with protein hazes, they should try increasing boiling times. Good advice given too late is bad advice.

<hr />

Only two people at Castle Eden were members of the Institute of Brewing; the General Manager, Brian Spencer, and myself. I was taken aback one day when Brian told me that the company was conducting a cost-cutting exercise and was aiming to reduce the number of professional subscriptions that it paid each year. The idea was that at each location, the most senior member of staff would retain their membership of the Institute and would circulate his copy of the 'Journal' to the others, who would no longer need to be members. For some reason, I agreed to comply with this without a second thought and in due course, sent in my letter of resignation.

When I received the reply from the Institute saying how sorry they were to be losing such a 'distinguished member', I began to realise what I had done. After all the effort and hard work it had taken for me to become a Diploma member, I was angry at the company for dismissing this so lightly. I wished that I had told them that I would pay the subscription out of my own pocket – it was only a matter of a few pounds but the deed was done and I let it lie. The only consolation was that I was still invited to the annual banquets of the Yorkshire and north-eastern section, which were held at the *Old Swan Hotel* in Harrogate.

I particularly enjoyed the Harrogate banquets because it gave me the chance to socialise with my old Yorkshire friends from Sheffield and Leeds. During one banquet around this time, I bumped into Alastair Ross who had been the Head Brewer and General Manager of Castle Eden when I had first started there. 'You're not still working for Whitbread's, are you?' he asked, in a jovial manner. After an evening of feasting and drinking, the atmosphere was very mellow and insults about each other's breweries were often good-humouredly cast around. We exchanged a few more remarks in a similar vein before parting on convivial terms.

The gist of what he had said was that changes were coming and that I ought to find a job with another company, before it was too late. Such was the atmosphere in which this conversation was carried out, that I took this to be the usual joking and allowed his words to disappear into the furthest, dark corners of my mind, where they remained for several years.

Holiday time again, but imagine my surprise when I returned, refreshed from my break, to find pickets on the brewery gate. Castle Eden was on strike. It had started in the distribution department and the whole workforce had come out in sympathy. The company had introduced a new type of delivery lorry which required pint cases to be stacked five high and half-pint cases, six high. The drivers believed that this was an unsafe arrangement; that bottles might fly off when they were negotiating the winding, undulating roads of their extensive delivery area. Because it was the individual drivers who would be held responsible if there had been an accident, they refused to implement the new system and in this they were supported by their union, the Transport and General Workers' Union. On the other hand, the local management had been told that these vehicles had to be introduced at Castle Eden since they had been accepted elsewhere in the group.

The crunch came when a fork-lift truck driver was instructed by management to load a lorry in the new configuration. At the same time, his union had told him to do no such thing. The hapless man had no choice but to refuse the management instruction. He was immediately suspended and the whole workforce, distribution and production walked out. It was at this stage that I had returned from my holidays.

Because it was a distribution matter, I was not involved in the negotiations, thank goodness. The production staff and myself rolled up our sleeves and made sure that all the beer in the brewery, which of course was at different stages of production, was secure, in good condition and ready for when the strike ended. In the meantime, the negotiations focused on the nature of trials to be carried out on the new lorries, which would be agreeable to management and would allay the fears of the drivers. After an eight day stoppage, agreement was reached and the men returned to work.

There seemed to be an unwritten inference that the responsibility for the strike lay with the local Castle Eden management and indeed, after a respectable period of time had passed, Brian Spencer, the General Manager, was transferred elsewhere in the region. From where I was standing it looked as though the Castle Eden management were taking their instructions from Regional Headquarters in Sheffield, but when the balloon went up the local men became the scapegoats.

Eventually, a director was sent to Castle Eden to run the site. The man appointed was Paul Cox, a thirty-year-old mathematics graduate whose last post had been Distribution Director of R. White and Sons, Whitbread's soft drinks subsidiary. He was a non-brewer and since I was the most senior brewer at Castle Eden and directly responsible for every aspect of production, I felt that I should be designated as Head Brewer. However, this was not to be. I was informed by the Regional Production Director that I would be known as the Senior Brewer. I concluded that the use of this non-title was rather petty, particularly as it would relieve the company of the obligation to give me a higher salary and a company car, the established rewards for Head Brewers. My respect for regional management was ebbing.

The new local director, Paul Cox, brought with him a new style of management. He brought to Castle Eden the concept of the site forum. The first one was held at Peterlee Catholic Club and all the Castle Eden employees and their families were invited. A handful of Whitbread directors attended and several regional and district Transport and General Workers' Union officials were also invited.

Paul Cox introduced the event and officially announced some startling changes that were going to take place in the brewery. However, the main theme of the forum was 'Industrial Democracy' and the first speaker on this subject was Joe Mills, the Regional Secretary for the Northern Region of the T & GWU, who called for companies to operate an 'open book situation'. The next speaker was Martin Findlay, Whitbread Group Personnel Director – the man responsible for the company's policy on industrial democracy. He said that the industrial democracy policy of a company was that it was there to ensure that all who worked for a company were fully involved in its business so far as it affected their own jobs. I felt that there was a certain irony about the situation in view of the fact that what Paul Cox had just announced was that the bottling department at Castle Eden was going to be closed down with the loss of thirteen jobs. So much for industrial democracy, I thought.

The bottling hall was to be demolished in order to make space for a substantial expansion of Castle Eden's kegging and filtration facilities so that Heineken lager, brewed at Whitbread's modern brewery at Salmesbury could be tankered up and processed and packaged locally. Many people were enthusiastic about the new changes; however, I had some reservations. The loss of bottling meant that we would also lose Mackeson brewing. Fortunately, the sales of ales at Castle Eden had increased every year that I had been there, which was perhaps against the national trend at that time. To be fair to him, Paul Cox conceded: 'that in recent months at Castle

Eden there had been a considerable slowing up in the rate of sales growth of lagers and a dramatic rise in the sales of Best Scotch Ale which was brewed at Castle Eden.'

Other repercussions of the loss of bottling were that the sale of Mackeson to Federation and Scottish and Newcastle Breweries would have to be supplied from further south, as would the supply of bottled Mackeson and Guinness to Castle Eden. The net result, it seemed to me, was that the changes would boost the brewing of Mackeson and possibly Heineken at other breweries, with the loss of over four hundred barrels a week of Mackeson brewing at Castle Eden. This did not seem to augur well for the long term future of Castle Eden as a brewery, as opposed to a processing or distribution centre. The company view was that new plant would mean continuing employment levels. Only time would tell if my fears were justified.

After the main speakers had finished, the floor was opened to the employees to ask questions. The brewery shop stewards, who could always be relied on to say something, asked three questions. As for the remainder of the 130–odd audience, there was no comment or question at all. Perhaps they were all impatient to get to the free buffet that the company had laid on.

⟫ ❍ ⟪

After the forum at Castle Eden, 'consultation', meetings became fashionable within the company. In the winter of 1978/9, I was invited to such a meeting in Sheffield, together with other production staff from the East-Pennines region who held similar positions to me. The meeting was held in the *Victoria Hotel,* which was adjacent to the old Victoria Railway Station and quite close to Tennant's Brewery by Lady's Bridge. A conference room had been made available for us and when we were all assembled one of the regional directors took the platform to address us. After all these years I cannot recall exactly how his presentation began, but I believe it followed the usual pattern: 'We find ourselves operating in a competitive market... the board is determined that we should succeed... we must become leaner and fitter to meet the challenge... difficult choices have to be made...', and then came the bombshell: 'in order to achieve this streamlining, the following people will be offered voluntary redundancy'.

The atmosphere became painfully tense as we listened in breathless silence as the list of names was read. A Yorkshire brewer, who I knew, stood up and protested when his name was called. I admired his spirit. But when my name was spoken, I could not move. I was stunned; I could not believe it. All the wind was taken out of my sails and I shrunk into myself.

Shortly after this, the meeting broke up for coffee and I felt the need to get away from the crowd. I walked out into the spacious foyer and found myself an isolated chair. My brain started working again and the thoughts raced through it like steam trains. I had given my whole life to brewing; working, playing and studying. I had lived for brewing, twenty-four hours a day and now it seemed it was all for nothing. How could they do that? Why? I became aware of two members of the Dubliners folk group (my all-time favourites) walking by. They must have been booked for one of the Sheffield theatres. Ronnie Drew's leg was in plaster and my world was coming to an end. It all seemed like a weird dream.

When I returned to Castle Eden, I reported to my colleagues what had been said at the meeting. Like me, they were stunned and incredulous. When it had all sunk in, some members of staff, understandably, became concerned about the security of their own jobs. Assistant Brewer Ian Butchers, who had recently taken over from Jack Reddy (who had moved on to Luton Brewery), made enquiries about his own future. He was told, rather abruptly, that nobody's job was guaranteed. Ian was married and had two young children. For once in my life, I was grateful that I was single.

After a few weeks, I was invited down to Chiswell Street Brewery, the company headquarters in London, to discuss my future. The meeting was arranged for mid-morning, but since I had never been there before I did not know how convenient it was to locate. It seemed a shame that the one and only chance I would get to see this historic site was under such depressing circumstances. When the day came, I caught the first train south which meant getting up at four o'clock in the morning. It arrived in London late so I got a taxi to the brewery, which seemed to take forever.

When I got to Chiswell Street, I was still late (and still angry). I found out where the meeting was to be held and ran up several flights of stairs to the place where two company directors were waiting impatiently for me. They asked me if I had decided what I wanted to do and, when I had got my breath back, I told them that I would be very happy to continue brewing at Castle Eden. One of them replied sharply that that was not an option and indeed, as the conversation went round in circles, no further options, other than redundancy, were offered. The meeting came to a close and a date was set when I must 'make up my mind'. I embarked on the return leg just as dejected as I had been on the outward journey.

After I had been back in Castle Eden a few weeks, the Personnel department informed me how much redundancy I would get, should I decide to accept it. The sum was just over thirteen thousand pounds, which, even in 1979, did not seem very generous to me for nearly twenty years professional service.

However, around that time, I received an invitation to visit Whitbread's Samlesbury Brewery near Preston, presumably with a view to employment possibilities. At least this was something positive. Samlesbury had been opened in 1972; it was enormous and modern. When I arrived there, I was given a tour around the site. There were rows of two thousand barrel conical fermenting vessels, one of which could have swallowed up the lion's share of a week's brewing at Castle Eden.

Everything was enclosed in stainless steel; I never saw so much as a splash of beer, wort or yeast anywhere. There was no chance of finding a hop 'lurking' here. Everything was automated and controlled via two large panels. Once the brewer had fed in his data, a single operator could activate and supervise the entire brewing process. The packaging hall was equally impressive. The two bottling lines were filling a thousand bottles a minute between them and the canning lines were working at twice that speed, such that the movement of the cans along the conveyors was just a blur to the naked eye.

After the tour, I was introduced to the Brewery Manager and he asked me about my professional history to date. As I described the small and medium sized breweries where I had worked (oak casks and vessels of copper and slate – breweries where, at every bend of the pipe, decisions had to be made by men of judgement and experience,) I had to acknowledge that we were operating in different worlds and mine was the one that I cherished and valued.

A few weeks later, I learned that they would not be offering me a post at Samlesbury and, in spite of my desperate situation, I was not disappointed by this news.

By now, it was clear that I had to make some sort of a decision, if only to preserve my own sanity. These days, I'm sure that doctors would have described my condition as 'suffering from stress' or even a minor breakdown but at that time, I did not visit doctors. I found myself, for the first and only time in my life, drinking to ease the pain, rather than for enjoyment and that was not good. I was determined, above everything else, that I should never again allow myself to be in the position where an employer could treat me in this way.

For a while, I considered the possibility of becoming self-sufficient – buying a small house with a piece of land and becoming dependent on no one. However, I did not think that such isolation from the world would have suited me. Around this time, my father died unexpectedly, plunging me even deeper into depression. He had enjoyed a mere eighteen months of retirement after a lifetime of hard work.

This reinforced my view that, in the prevailing political climate, loyalty to a company was misplaced – looking out for oneself was the order of the day. It was in this frame of mind that I decided to take the redundancy and get out.

I stipulated that I would work until the end of August, which was some months ahead. This would ensure that I completed twenty years service with the company and would therefore be eligible for the twenty-year pocket watch that I had long looked forward to. It was evident that the brewing industry was contracting and it was unlikely that I would be able to get another job there.

In 1979, there were no jobs of any kind to be had anywhere – least of all in the north-east of England. However, I was still under forty-years-of-age, I was single and I still had a brain in my head. Perhaps I could turn this disaster into an opportunity for a new start – a new direction.

⟫ ❍ ⟪

One evening, I had called into the brewery as usual to check that all was well and that all the night shift had arrived when a rather strange experience occurred. Some of the fermentations were at the stage when they needed the yeast heads stripping off and in consequence, the men were far too busy to join me for a night cap on this occasion.

Instead of wandering down to the Wet Canteen, I thought I would have a 'quickie' in *Grufferty's Bar*, while I still could. This gentle haven was soon to be demolished to make way for the new processing plant. I poured myself a drink and sat with it at the bar rather wearily – I had not been sleeping very well. In the subdued lighting, I became aware of the face of William Nimmo looking at me from the corner of the room. It was the same sad face that looked down from his portrait in the brewery reception. I brushed it off as a consequence of my mental and emotional exhaustion but, if I had been a superstitious man, I might have thought that I had seen a ghost. *Grufferty's Bar* had been built on the part of the site where, many years before, the old man's ashes had been scattered.

Thankfully, it was not all gloom and doom at this time. I was still to enjoy one more brewing highlight, albeit short-lived, before I left. We had a new General Manager, (Paul Cox had moved on to become Operations Director-North). The new manager was Peter Symes, a jovial and sociable man. He went out of his way to express sympathy about the way the company had treated me, which I appreciated and which reassured me that I was not becoming paranoid.

One day he came to me and asked if it would be possible for me to carry out trails and produce a new beer at Castle Eden without the knowledge of my regional bosses in Sheffield. I told him that I could; after all we had the small, slate fermenting vessels of twenty to thirty barrel capacity which were ideal for such trails, but what was I to do if one of the Sheffield directors rang me up and asked me point blank if I was brewing a new beer? 'Just do a Basil Fawlty,' he said, 'and pretend to have a heart attack on the end of the phone!' I was going to enjoy working with this man.

In the north-east, there was a beer sold in Workingmen's Clubs known generally as 'Ordinary'. Its main characteristic was that it was very cheap to buy, which by implication meant that it was a low gravity beer. It was drunk mostly by the elderly and by the unemployed; the elderly, who could not take the more potent beers and the unemployed who could not afford them. Thus a man drinking Ordinary could keep up with the more affluent young bucks without losing face.

Several breweries in the region produced an Ordinary, but we did not; it was this omission that Peter Symes wished to remedy, particularly as the club trade was an area where there was scope for us to expand into.

I carried out a certain amount of 'consumer research' on our

Beer mats: 'My' brew - Castle Keep, and old Nimmo's era mat and a Tennant's Gold Label mat from Sheffield.

competitors' products and then set about creating a new beer. It was rare for a brewer to get such a chance and even though Ordinary was a rather lowly product, I was grateful to Peter for this unique opportunity.

The main challenge in formulating such a beer was to achieve the 'meat and tatties' fullness in such a low gravity beer. Weak beers generally drank very 'thin', but the men of the north-east sought more full-bodied flavours. I approached this problem in two ways; firstly in the fermenting vessel. By judicious cooling, I stopped the fermentation a little earlier than usual so that sufficient un-fermented material remained in the beer to give it a malty smoothness. The second modification came in the cellar, where I increased the priming rate. This meant that I was adding extra brewing syrups to the finished beer.

The result of my efforts was a low gravity beer with a balanced and uncharacteristically full flavour. It was independently tested on a sample population in the region and the results were very favourable.

At the beginning of August it went on general sale, followed by an advertising campaign involving T.V. commercials, local radio and newspapers. The launch was organised by a London-based marketing company. They had decided to call the beer, Castle Keep, a name that I felt did not relate very strongly to our target market, the unemployed and the elderly. I had suggested Extra-Ordinary. However, such was my enthusiasm for the project, they could have called it anything and I would have been happy.

(The company had a tendency to use London-based marketing and advertising agencies for their products – even in the far-flung regions. A year or so earlier, a large advertising hoarding had been placed at the approaches to Middlesbrough, sporting the motto – TROPHY - THE BEER WE DRINK ON *TEESIDE*. No doubt our competitors were amused by the misspelling.)

As a postscript to the Castle Keep story: not long before I left, I was tasting the beers in the sample room when I noticed that the Castle Keep was not quite right. It had a hint of that thinness that I had been at pains to avoid. I asked the cellar foreman if it had been primed at the specified rate and he informed me that the primings had been reduced on the instructions of the 'new brewer'.

The 'new brewer' was a man from the South of England whom the company had recently sent to Castle Eden to replace me. (He was to have the title of Head Brewer and had a company car.) I sought him out and asked him why the primings had been reduced. He said that he had found the beer rather sweet. I did not feel inclined to explain to him the pains that I had gone to, to match the flavour of the beer to local tastes rather than to the preferences of those from other parts of the country. I just turned on my heels and walked away. I had done my best and soon I would be gone.

As my leaving day approached, I was inundated with invitations to farewell parties and presentations from my friends and colleagues at the brewery – not only the production staff but also the foremen, the Excise Officer, the Sales department, Wages, the brewery men, Dad's Army and many more. I received some wonderful gifts, too many to itemize them all, but I must mention a couple. Dad's Army presented me with a wonderful Combined Services shield, hand painted by Harry Bartlett, the sign writer and inscribed – 'To Frank Priestley from Dad's Army'. It still holds pride of place in my house today. Peter Symes gave me a framed poster advertising Castle Keep. It had been personalised by the addition of the words, 'Thanks to Frank Priestley.' I also finally got my twenty-year pocket watch from the company.

The parties and drinking sessions followed one after another so that by the time that I actually left, I was just about 'partied out'. But not before, on more than one occasion, I had sung a few verses from the old, traditional song, *The Parting Glass,* as my way of saying thank you and farewell. The first verse is shown below:

Of all the money that e'er I had,
I spent it in good company.
And all the harm I've ever done,
Alas! It was to none but me.
And all I've done for want of wit,
To mem'ry now I can't recall.
So fill to me the parting glass,
Good night and joy be with you all.

For the first few days it was like a holiday, having no work to go to, but very soon I was missing the brewery – missing the sight, sound and smell of the brewery. But even more than that, I was missing the fellowship of my colleagues; the sorting out of problems, the passing the time of day, the laughter and the jokes. As that old-time Exciseman, Robert Burns wrote in *A Bottle and a Friend*:

Here's a bottle and an honest friend!
What wad ye wish for mair, man?
Wha kens, before his life may end,
What his share may be of care, man?

Then catch the moments as they fly,
And use them as ye ought, man:
Believe me, happiness is shy,
And comes not ay when sought, man.

As anticipated, I could not get a job, of any kind. I spent my time walking around and I took the opportunity to do more writing. I wrote a novel called, *The Drowning Man*. Its main character (surprise, surprise) was a brewer who had been made redundant after twenty years service.

Unsurprisingly, I could not find a publisher for this depressing tale but it did benefit me in another way. I was beginning to find that creative writing was therapeutic. By raking over the most desperate episodes of my life and setting them down on paper, I was, in some way, writing the pain out of my system. I started to make plans. Reluctantly, I had to accept that there was no future for me in the north-east at that time. The unemployment rate was amongst the highest in the land. I decided to move down to the Peak District of Derbyshire, close to my mother to my two brothers who both lived on the western edges of our home town, Sheffield. I hoped that I would be able to make a new start there.

10

The Rainbow

It took me more than a year to sell my house in Elwick and move down to Derbyshire and when I landed there, I discovered that the job situation was no better than in the north-east. I had been unemployed for long enough and after a great deal of soul searching, I decided to go to college and train to be a science teacher. I was already well-versed in biology and biochemistry and I believed that I would gain some satisfaction from imparting knowledge to eager young minds. Not only that, but in those days I would get a generous grant which would more than cover my college and living expenses.

In the summer of 1981, I enrolled on a B.Ed. course in Biology at the local College of Higher Education which was situated in the Derbyshire town of Matlock. The question arose, would I, as a mature student, be able to keep up with the eighteen year-olds, when it came to assignments and examinations? I resisted the temptation to claim that I could pass anything – except a pub; because embellishing my route home from the college, a walk that could take anything from thirty minutes onwards, was a succession of public houses, named in the traditional manner, after trees.

There was *The Thorntree, The Sycamore, The Crabtree,* (later changed to *the Willows*), *The Laburnum* and finally *The Holly Bush*. I am not suggesting that all these establishments dated back to the days of taverns and ale houses; it was much more likely that they were named after prominent trees that happened to be growing nearby, on the south facing slopes of this fertile valley.

Three years later, I had an Education degree and met Jane, a fellow student who had agreed to become my wife. We were married in 1984 at All Saints Church in Matlock. Before the ceremony, I called into *The Duke of Wellington* pub for a little 'fortification' in preparation for this momentous act. Some of my future in-laws were already there – presumably also getting 'fortified'. One of them spotted me and called across, 'Is that Frank Priestley over there?' Whereupon, a head popped up from behind the bar and exclaimed, 'Did somebody say Frank Priestley?' It was Eric Cooper, who had been a cooper at the Sheffield brewery when I worked there. I had not seen him for more than ten years but in the meantime he had retrained and was now employed servicing beer dispensing equipment. Seeing Eric after all those years recalled the days of Tennant's Brewery and was an excellent omen for my marriage.

It was a strange irony that when I acquired an education qualification, there were next-to-no jobs in Secondary teaching available – not even for science teachers. However, I was not down-hearted; 12 weeks or so of teaching practice had modified my idealistic view of teaching as 'imparting knowledge to eager young minds'. Since my own school days, strict discipline and the means of maintaining it had been abandoned in favour of more progressive ideas and I now felt that the working conditions in the average Comprehensive classroom were not as attractive as I had anticipated.

However, I had responsibilities now; I had a wife and we were keen to start a family as soon as possible. I took any job that I could get and in any location. We even moved back to the north-east briefly, to the village of Sedgefield in County Durham. The village, or more accurately, the market town, was built around a large, picturesque green which was dominated by the imposing fifteen century tower of St Edmund's Church. Around the green was an interesting variety of public houses – *The Golden Lion, The*

Dun Cow Inn, Hope Inn, The Black Lion and just in view of the green, *The Hardwick Arms*. Between the *Hope Inn* and the church was the site of Cooper's Almshouses, which unfortunately had been demolished in 1969. The locals knew this area as 'Faith, Hope and Charity'. The next pub along the green was the *Dun Cow*; this was where the then-Prime Minister, Tony Blair took tee-totaller, George W. Bush for a 'drink'. But much more importantly, it was where I celebrated after the birth of my first son, Daniel in 1986.

The range of jobs that I took on included some work in industry but they were mostly slanted towards training, tutoring or some aspect of education. The twenty years after leaving college saw me in eleven different jobs.

By 1987, we had moved back to Derbyshire, to the former lead mining town of Wirksworth, which has now become our permanent home. It proved to be an appropriate location, reflecting, as it did, many of my cherished interests. Nestling beneath a hill called Barrel Edge, the town had once supported more than fifty ale houses and inns – the old miners believed that generous intakes of ale were a necessary antidote to the lead poisoning that was associated with their occupation. Many of the pubs had brewed

Wirksworth town

their own beer and consequently, coopers and maltsters had done business in the town. However, when we arrived on the scene, the number of pubs had shrunk to nine, but this still offered an interesting choice of drinking holes in a town with a population of a mere six thousand souls.

The Parish Room, near the church, had originally been a malt office but was later converted into a wines and spirits warehouse and at one time Wirksworth had had its own whisky blender and bottler. The firm of Charles Wright & Sons, established in 1795, had bottled two brands of whisky; Glen Haddon, a seven year old malt and Old Gran which was ten years old. The business had continued up until 1962, when the premises were converted into a public house – *The Vaults*. A preserved poster advertising Old Gran can still be seen in the main lounge of the pub. I am happy to report that a 'Wirksworth Whisky' bottle has recently come into my possession; the sad news is that the bottle is completely empty.

In recent years, I have taken an increasing interest in whisky production; after all, a distillery is just a brewery producing un-hopped ale with a still tacked on to the end of the line. Whereas mashing and fermentation are the critical stages of ale brewing, I believe the still man and the blender are the key posts in a distillery. I have visited such establishments both in Scotland and in Ireland and I have enjoyed their 'fruits' in equal measure. (I have yet to visit the new one in Penderyn, Wales and sample some Welsh whisky.) My wife is half Scottish whilst I am a quarter Irish. Over the years, it has given me mischievous pleasure to remind her Caledonian relations that the 'water of life' was invented in Ireland and only later did its secrets become known in Scotland, probably via some much-travelled and talkative Irish monk.

But back to Wirksworth; on the day we moved in to the town, the first pub that we visited, while we were waiting for the key to the new house, was *The Black's Head*. It was a snug little retreat, situated in the corner of the Market Place and probably dating from the early 1700s. Although its clientele included young people and contemporary music played in the background, the old fireplaces and beams gave it an intimacy that made it easy to imagine how it had been in centuries past when its main customers would have been miners and quarrymen, eager to quench their thirsts. It was these thoughts that prompted me to write the poem, *Going Back,* which was published in several anthologies.

Sitting in the cranium of the ethnic minority.
Listening to the sound of the silent majority.
Drowned by the tapes that are almost the rage.
The under-young man slowly grows over-age.

Climbing the cobbled lane to the ale house door.
The old man shuffles in, ruffling sawdust on the floor.
Smell of clay pipe, quarry dust on his coat.
The click of shove-ha'penny, chewed tobacco in the throat.

The squeezebox of time plays yet another song.
As the wide years contract and short cancels long.
The traveller returns as the generations shrink.
Back in the Black's Head, he smiles himself a drink.

The Black's Head became one of my regular 'locals' and at one time, they had a barmaid there who became very accomplished at anticipating my every (drinking) need. I only had to smile at her across the room and she would pour my next drink, which at that house was a glass of Hardy Hanson bitter chased by a Bell's whisky, which explains the line, 'he smiles himself a drink.' Recently, the pub has come under new management and the old inn sign with its smiling black face, welcoming those of taste and thirst through its portal, has been removed from the front of the building and replaced by something much more politically correct, displaying no such traditional image.

Next to *The Black's Head* stands *The Crown Inn*, a former

coaching inn dating from around 1745. It is no longer a hostelry, but the carriage arch remains. Baroness Orczy, author of *The Scarlet Pimpernel,* featured *The Crown Inn* in her novel, *Beau Brocade.* Three miles south of Wirksworth, in the village of Idridgehay, stands *The Black Swan*, another pub with literary connections. George Elliot often visited her relations in Wirksworth and used the town for much of the setting for her novel, *Adam Bede*. The disreputable tavern in the story, *The Wagon Overthrown*, was based on *The Black Swan*. I must hasten to point out that *The Black Swan* is no longer disreputable (if it ever was) and is nowadays an excellent pub for eating, drinking and being entertained.

A further three miles down the road towards Belper, stands the 350-year-old *Hanging Gate* pub at Shottle. As the name suggests, it has a gate as a sign, hanging high up so that it does not impede the progress of thirsty customers into the pub. It used to have the following verse painted on its staves, the poem is now displayed inside the pub:

> *This gate hangs well*
> *And Hinders none*
> *Refresh and pay*
> *And Travel on*
> > G.H. Flint

Another local pub with an interesting sign is the 17th century coaching inn, *The Green Man*, situated in the market town of Ashbourne, eight miles south-west of Wirksworth. The sign is one of those which extend all the way across the main road to form an archway. It was constructed to commemorate the amalgamation of two coaching inns in 1825 when the pub became *The Green Man* and *The Black's Head*. H.R.H. Prince Charles, Prince of Wales recently called in to the pub for a tot of malt whisky before starting the 2003 Shrovetide football game. Ashbourne (like Sedgefield) still plays this ancient game where half the town takes on the other half, with a minimum of rules. The origins of the Ashbourne game are so remote that in the distant past it may have been played with a human head (or so it is claimed). That's *real* football.

The highest pub in Derbyshire is the four hundred year old Barrel at Bretton which stands at 1,250 feet above sea level. My brothers took me there on my stag night in 1984. It had a wonderful atmosphere and was a good pub to get high in. The oldest pub in the county town is *The Dolphin*, which stands in sight of Derby Cathedral. The beamed bar dates back to 1530 and it is claimed that a corridor in the inn was once a narrow medieval street. It was in the city of Derby that my second son John was born in 1989.

Crossing the county border into Nottinghamshire, there is one of the handful of pubs which claim to be the oldest in England. *Ye Olde Trip to Jerusalem*, dating from 1189, is situated in an area known as Brewhouse Yard, beneath the castle rock in Nottingham. It is believed to have been a collecting point for Crusaders and pilgrims to refresh themselves before the long journey to the Holy Land. Part of the pub extends into the ancient caves in the rock face and tunnels from the bar lead up to the castle above.

It is interesting to recall that the town of Nottingham had been founded in the 6th century by an Anglo-Saxon with the unfortunate name of 'Snot'. The settlement he established was named after him and was originally called Snotengaham. You can hardly blame the locals for subsequently changing it to Nottingham.

Moving swiftly north to Yorkshire, the oldest pub in Sheffield, the town of my birth, is the *Old Queen's Head* on Pond Street. It dates back to the 15th century but now finds itself part of a modern bus station. It is reputed to be haunted, but I have only encountered friendly spirits there.

Any amble through memorable pubs, however brief, would not be complete without a mention of Ireland. The oldest pub in that magical country is the *Brazen Head* on Bridge Street in Dublin. It has been trading for eight hundred years and stands on the site of a 12th century tavern near the River Liffey. In common with many

Irish pubs, the impression is given that the ambience and furnishings have changed very little over the centuries – so much so that it is easy to imagine the days gone by when its convivial atmosphere attracted smugglers, merchants, rebels and patriots including such leading figures in Ireland's quest for independence as Wolfe Tone, Daniel O'Connell and Robert Emmet. The writing desk used by Emmet is still on the premises and it is said that the *Brazen Head* was the last place that he had a drink before his abortive rebellion. Enthusiastic drinkers have claimed to have seen his ghost after a long night.

The *Brazen Head* features in many tourist guides but one Irish pub that I came upon purely by chance was Paddy Linehan's *Moby Dick* in Youghal on the south coast of Co. Cork. This location was chosen for the setting of the film, Moby Dick, which starred Gregory Peck as Captain Ahab. It seems that many of those involved in the film enjoyed the hospitality of this convivial hostelry.

Leo Genn, the actor is quoted as saying:

'To Paddy Linehan,

A better Mayor than Raleigh, a better poet than Spenser, and the best barman of them all.'

And from John Huston, the director:

'To Paddy Linehan, under whose roof I found comfort and warmth.'

The oldest pub in Sheffield: The Old Queen's Head, as it was in the 1960s.

After enjoying a few pints of Murphy's there, I was in no position to contradict them.

These are just a handful out the many hundreds of pubs I must have visited in my lifetime. Any drinking man could produce a similar list (probably longer) outlining some of his favourites and some that recall the memorable highlights of his life. The public houses of the British Isles are a unique and priceless asset; from comfortable country inns to ancient village pubs; from the ornate Victorian town-centre pubs to snug locals on the corners of terraced streets. These, together with the more recent additions, offer the tippler an endless opportunity for exploration, discovery and enjoyment. It is worth looking back in history to find out how this resource, unequalled in other lands, came into being.

When the Romans arrived on our shores they found that the ancient Britons were already well versed in the brewing and drinking of alcoholic beverages and they noted that they were 'very quarrelsome in their cups'. In fact, Britain's first known brewer, Atrectus the Brewer, had his name inscribed on a wooden leaf tablet at the Vindolanda fort on Hadrian's Wall in the second century. The Britons brewed some ale together with mead and cider, which were probably produced and drunk on their homesteads. It is the Romans we have to thank for establishing the first drinking houses. They set up *tabernae vineriae* or wine shops at regular intervals along the new roads they were building. These *tabernae* served wine and food which customers consumed around a communal table.

After the Romans left, the cultivation of vines declined and the population reverted to ale drinking once again. In 688AD, King Ina of Wessex made laws setting up alehouses to replace the Roman *tabernae*. Alehouses, sometimes known as tipple houses, brewed and sold ale (later beer) on the premises. The ale was usually brewed by the woman of the house, as an extension of the cooking – thus the name brewster. One can quite imagine that where a brewster was good at her art, the room of her house she kept open to the public would be buzzing with stories and songs of drinkers who had happily gathered there – the true forerunner of the public house.

The Angles, Saxons and Vikings who followed the Romans were all enthusiastic ale drinkers and the alehouses must have attracted much lively custom. So much so that the Saxon King Edgar (959-75), under the influence of St Dunstan, closed down many, limiting small towns and villages to just one such alehouse.

He also enforced the use of cups with pegs down the side of them so that, 'what person drank past the pins in one draught should forfeit a penny.' This gave rise to the phrase, 'take him down a peg or two.' The King's efforts to curtail drinking, like so many such measures since, seemed to have been counter-productive. Drinkers began to use the pegged cups in competitions to find out who could drink the fastest. Today, the village pub can be seen as the descendant of the alehouse.

In the towns around the land, taverns could be found. These were the urban equivalent of the alehouse. Taverns, like alehouses, were open to the public and in addition to ale served other drinks such as wine and cider as well as food. They became convivial meeting places where townsmen could enjoy pleasant refreshment in good company. Like alehouses, they could only open during set hours; restricted hours had been imposed since 1329, to deny criminal elements a place to hide.

In the Middle Ages, monasteries were obliged by their rules to provide food and shelter to travellers in need, such as pilgrims. Although the accommodation was usually rather basic, monasteries had their own brewhouses so doubtless a good drink of ale would have helped the travellers sleep on the rush-strewn floors. As already mentioned, it was the monks of Burton Abbey, founded in 1002AD, who largely established that town as a centre for brewing excellence. In addition to these monastic hospices, similar establishments were attached to the castles of the nobility. Together, these were the earliest inns and today, some of the oldest surviving pubs can trace their origins to these ancient hostelries (e.g. *Ye Olde Trip to Jerusalem*).

These early inns with their austere dormitories were soon overtaken by commercial establishments which could offer more comfortable facilities. Inns provided food, drink and accommodation to bona fide travellers and were consequently permitted to remain open at any hour. They were not, however, allowed to serve local drinkers – as a result, they often had taverns attached, in order to remedy this situation.

During the 15th and 16th centuries, the amount of travelling increased and this was reflected in the number and quality of inns around the country. By the 17th century, when the 1663 Turnpike Act resulted in improved roads, the network of coaching inns every fifteen miles or so along the roads, became more fully established. They provided a change of horses, food and drink for the passengers and comfortable accommodation at night.

One of the finest I've seen, that still survives, is *The George* at Stamford in Lincolnshire. Situated strategically between London and York, it became one of the most famous coaching inns in England. On either side of the entrance hall are the old waiting rooms, still named 'York' and 'London' for the use of passengers seeking those destinations. The inn also displays a 'gallows' style inn sign, stretching all the way across the main road, the old Great North Road.

By the 18th century, mail was also being carried by coach and this period was, without doubt, the golden age of the coaching inn, but it was not to last. The 19th century saw the advent of the railways and this swifter form of travel marked a decline in the old coaching inns. However, there sprung up around the country hostelries with names like *Station Hotel* and *Railway Inn* to service this latest form of transport, just as a century before the building of the canal system had brought forth pubs with names like *Navigation*, *Boat* and *Barge*.

The Industrial Revolution marked two significant developments in our pubs. As droves of workers migrated from the countryside to the towns, accommodation had to be provided for them. Streets of small terraced houses were rapidly built around our expanding towns and on almost every street corner a pub was built. These became the 'village pubs' of the suburbs and quickly became the social centres of the new communities.

The second change was more fundamental. Whereas previously most pubs had brewed their own beer, trade was now so great as to make this more difficult. Numerous specialist brewers became established to satisfy the growing demand and drinkers became familiar with such names as Whitbread, Bass and Watney. In order to consolidate their position, these new brewers bought up outlets for their beers and tied others to sell only their products by making favourable financial deals with them. The advantages of this system were firstly, the breweries had the resources and the motivation of competition to refurbish the pubs and make them comfortable and attractive places in which to relax. Secondly, it was in the brewers' interest to train the publicans in the art of cellar work and, by regular inspections, ensure that the pint that was served over the bar was as good as that drawn in the brewery sample room.

In the 20th century, an increasing number of our pubs were becoming tied to a small number of large brewery groups. This resulted in a situation where in many areas a drinker's choice was confined to the products of just one or two brewers. An attempt to remedy this was made in 1990, when the Beer Orders forced the large brewers to sell off some of their pubs in areas where a monopoly existed. It was intended to increase the number of free houses; however, many of these establishments were bought up by the newly emerging pub groups. I was not impressed with my first experience of one such pub, but that may have been largely due to my own prejudice, with a publican apparently operating without the technical support of a brewery. Since then, I have visited many large pub-group pubs in towns and cities and found them offering a wide selection of regional and small-brewery beers, serving them in good condition and at very competitive prices.

Another spin-off from the Beer Orders was that the big brewers were required to 'put on tap' at least one traditional draught beer, as a guest beer, from a source other than their own breweries. In general, this was a good idea, provided that the turnover of this additional brand was high enough to ensure that its good condition was maintained – cask conditioned beer has a relatively short shelf life.

Today, the differences between alehouses, taverns and inns has become largely blurred and although country inns were abandoned in favour of the railways and many of the customers of the village pubs fled to find work in the towns, the motor car has ensured that those rural hostelries that have survived are now sought after and cherished as part of the rich spectrum of public houses across the land.

As Dr. Johnson said: '...there is nothing which has yet been contrived by man, by which so much happiness is produced, as by a good tavern or inn.'

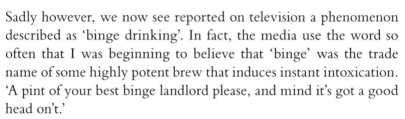

Sadly however, we now see reported on television a phenomenon described as 'binge drinking'. In fact, the media use the word so often that I was beginning to believe that 'binge' was the trade name of some highly potent brew that induces instant intoxication. 'A pint of your best binge landlord please, and mind it's got a good head on't.'

Drinkers of my age (the grumpy old sods generation) have always taken pride in the belief that we could 'take our ale'. Our aim has been to keep up with the next man whilst retaining some semblance (however flimsy) of sobriety. If a man could not hold his drink, it was considered as a stain upon his character. However, some of today's young drinkers do not seem concerned about stains on their characters, or on anything else for that matter. Their aim is to get disgustingly drunk as quickly as possible and to be seen to have done so. I am not suggesting that this generation invented drunkenness. Many of us have made our way homewards in the manner of blind donkeys – but none of us would boast about it.

At a time when there has never been such a fine choice of quality alcoholic beverages within reach of the tippler, it is an sad irony that these immature drinkers, heedless of the awful consequences of mixing the grape with the barley, swill back a lethal combination of cheap wine, lager, alcopops and 'shots' of characterless spirits in their headlong rush to erode their sobriety and dignity.

There is one consolation from all this: the extensive selections of excellent draught, bottled ales (which my son calls, 'old men's beer') and fine malt whiskies which are now available, are ignored by the bingeing hordes and remain reserved for the delectation of civilised drinkers, amongst whose number I count myself.

━━◗ ◉ ◖━━

It is now 30 years since I worked in the breweries. It would be nice to think that those grand old palaces of copper, wood and slate had survived as well as I have – but I am afraid they have not. Bentley's Yorkshire Brewery at Woodlesford is now a housing estate. Only the maltings building remains to give some clue as to what stood there. Leeds City Council has erected a plaque on the site to inform the new residents and I am proud to say that some of my writing has been incorporated in it. Kirkstall Brewery has been converted into student accommodation and there is now a housing development on the site of wonderful Castle Eden Brewery. When I last visited Sheffield, I found that the 'extensive and handsome brewery' of Tennant Brothers had been razed to the ground. They are lost and gone forever.

But how has the industry in general fared? In the 1960s, the seven major brewery companies, Bass, Allied, Whitbread, Watney, Scottish and Newcastle, Courage and Guinness produced 73% of the total beer production, while the remaining 27% of beer was produced by 104 breweries. The big companies' strength lay in the substantial base of tied outlets that they maintained, but with the introduction of the afore-mentioned 1990 Beer Orders, all this was to change – probably more than most people had anticipated. More than ten thousand pubs were sold off – that is one in six of the country's hostelries – and this resulted in a substantial shake-up of the big companies.

Some of them, like Allied and Bass, have sold off their brewing interests and others, like Scottish and Newcastle, are selling their pubs. Whitbread has sold off its pubs and its brewing business to concentrate on hotels, restaurants and leisure clubs and I believe that very soon Guinness will no longer be brewing stout in the UK and already Newcastle Brown is no longer brewed in Newcastle. How amazing! 'Tadcaster Brown' doesn't have the same ring about it.

However, judging from the choice and quality of draught and bottled beers available today, I get the impression that those small and medium-sized breweries that have managed to survive the turmoil of the last fifty years, are thriving and are producing some distinctive beers of quality. Not only that, but micro-breweries seem to be sprouting up all over the place, brewing some interesting regional beers. It is a satisfying irony that they have brought us back full circle to the kitchen brewing of the Saxon brewsters.

Once we were settled in Wirksworth, I wrote a third novel, *Summer Snow*. The story was set in the near-future when the worst predictions of the effects of global warming had been realised. Publishers were not impressed with this doom-laden tome and like the first two efforts, it was rejected. Later, my prophesies on climatic instability began to be fulfilled, but by then the novel was 'old hat'. I finally began to accept what I had been hearing for some years; unless you have a famous name, it is statistically almost impossible to get a first novel published. There are thousands of other people trying to do the same thing; to be successful, you have to write something unique, that few others are in a position to attempt. With this in mind, I set about writing the history of Wirksworth. Not only is it a town with a long history, it is rather out of the way, being accessible only via two 'B' roads and because of this, much of its heritage remains unspoilt. I was able to find a publisher for the book without too much difficulty and in 2003, *The Wirksworth Saga – A short history over the last 300 million years*, was launched. This success prompted me to start writing, *The Brewer's Tale*.

When I was Senior Brewer at Castle Eden, I was 'the man', known and respected inside and outside the brewery. People used to hand me cigars (those were the days when it was OK to smoke cigars). The events of 1979 destroyed all that and did not do a deal for my self-esteem either. But now, thirty years later, I have a good wife, two fine sons and a couple of published books under my belt. I am in serious danger of finally becoming fulfilled.

As I sit here in the *Royal Oak*, one of my locals on the north end of town, enjoying a glass of Timothy Taylor's Landlord Ale and a dram of Black Bush from the world's oldest whiskey distillery, my eyes come to rest upon two posters on the wall, recommending the wares of long-forgotten breweries. The first advertises Pale, Mild and Strong Ales brewed at Eaton's Brewery, Cavendish Bridge and the second, Nut Brown Ales brewed at Offiler's Brewery, Derby. There is a third poster, which like a premonition advertises Bass of Burton, for at the time of drinking the red triangle no longer smiles over Burton town.

My thoughts drift back to my breweries and to *The Vaults* and *Brown's Bar*, to Hoylandswaine and *The Lady's Bridge*, to *Grufferty's Bar* and the Wet Canteen, to Nimmo's Social Club and Dad's Army, where, between those precious pints, there was conversation and songs, friendship and jokes, music and laughter and such magic that sober men could never dream of.

Index

Index